The Little Book Of C

Huw Collingbourne

bitwise books

The Little Book Of C

ISBN: 978-1-913132-04-0

bitwise books is an imprint of **dark neon**

written by
Huw Collingbourne

DOWNLOAD THE SOURCE CODE
All the source code of the examples in this book may be downloaded (free) from the publisher's web site:
http://www.bitwisebooks.com/

Contents

Introduction

C is one of the most important of all programming languages. But it can be quite hard to learn. And what's more, C programs are very easy to crash. That's because C gives the programmer the freedom to do all kinds of operations that other languages such as Java, Python or C# would never allow.

In the hands of a good programmer, C is an amazingly powerful language. In the hands of a not-so-good programmer, it is a disaster waiting to happen.

In this book, my aim is to guide you towards becoming a good C programmer. I'll do that as quickly as I can. I won't try to describe everything about the C language. There are plenty of references online that will do that. Instead, I will focus on all the things that you really need to know to write C programs that work.

What is C Used For?

The C language is used to program all kinds of different applications on all kinds of different platforms. It is used for building desktop applications, compilers, tools and utilities and even hardware devices such as microcontrollers which need the speed and efficiency for which C is designed.

Download the Source Code

All the source code shown in this book is available for download. The code can be used with any standard C compiler and it may be edited with any programming editor that supports the C language. For the convenience of Visual Studio users, the source code Zip archive contains code in the form of a single Visual Studio multi-project solution.

Download the code from the Bitwise Books web site at:

www.bitwisebooks.com

What is in This Book?

This book begins with a gentle introduction to C. Then it quickly moves on to more demanding topics: everything from C's 'scoping' rules to the important (but frequently misunderstood) connection between arrays and memory addresses. By the end of the book you will have a deep understanding both of the C language itself and also of the underlying 'architecture' of your computer.

Who Should Read This Book?

This book is suitable for both beginners and more experienced programmers switching to C from some other language such as Java, Ruby or Python. It doesn't matter which operating system you are using; there are C compilers for all major operating systems and once you learn to program C on one platform it will be fairly simple to program C on some other platform.

Making Sense of the Text

In this book, any C source code is written like this:

```
int add(int num1, int num2) {
    num1 = num1 + num2;
    return num1;
}
```

Sometimes when a string is too long to fit onto the width of the page in this book, I split over multiple lines using the \ character like this:

```
printf("Here I am displaying a very long string on \
screen, followed by a carriage return\n");
```

The \ character is valid in C as a way of continuing a string onto the next line. In some cases, the \ character may be shown in the listings in the book even though it is not used in the source code archive. That's simply for the sake of readability. It's up to you whether or not you split long strings over multiple lines in your own code.

Any output that you may expect to see on screen when a program is run is shown like this:

```
The result of that calculation is 24!
```

When there is a sample program to accompany the code, the program name is shown above the code like this:

HelloWorld

```
// program code shown here
```

Explanatory notes (which generally provide some hints or give a more in-depth explanation of some point mentioned in the text) are shown in a box like this:

Important

This is an explanatory note. You can skip it if you like – but if you do so, you may miss something of interest!

About the Author

Huw Collingbourne has been a programmer for more than 30 years. He is an online programming instructor with successful courses on C, C#, Java, Object Pascal, Ruby, JavaScript and other topics. For a full list of available courses be sure to visit the Bitwise Courses web site: http://bitwisecourses.com/

He is author of *The Book Of Ruby* from No Starch Press. He is a well-known technology writer in the UK and has written numerous opinion and programming columns for a number of computer magazines, such as Computer Shopper, PC Pro, and PC Plus.

At various times Huw has been a magazine publisher, editor, and TV broadcaster. He has an MA in English from the University of Cambridge and holds a 2nd dan black belt in aikido, a martial art which he teaches in North Devon, UK. The aikido comes in useful when trying to keep his Pyrenean Mountain Dogs under some semblance of control.

About the Technical Editor

Dr. Dermot Hogan is a software developer who has led major projects written in Assembly Language, C , C# and a number of other programming languages. A specialist in real time trading technologies, he has managed and developed global risk management systems for several international banks and financial institutions. He is the lead developer of the independent software company, SapphireSteel Software. He holds a Ph.D in physics from the University of Cambridge. His current area of research is devoted to robotic control and imaging systems.

1 – Getting Started

What sort of language is C and what software do you need in order to write, build and run C programs? This chapter explains how to get up and running with C programming and also how you should use this book when learning C.

C is a general-purpose compiled programming language. It was first developed by Dennis Ritchie in the late '60s and early '70s. The C language is used for all kinds of programming: everything from small utilities to complete applications, compilers and operating systems. The C language is also widely used for programming microcontrollers for hardware devices.

What is the C compiler?

A C compiler (and an associated tool called a 'linker') is the program that translates your source code (the text you write in an editor) into machine code that is capable of being run by your operating system. C compilers are available for all major operating systems including Windows, macOS and Linux.

Editors and IDEs

In order to write C code you will need a programming editor or IDE (Integrated Development Environment) and a C compiler. You will find links to some editors and compilers (many of which are free) in the Appendix of this book.

How Should You Study the Book?

The Little Book Of C starts by explaining the basic building blocks of C programming. In the early chapters I will explain everything you need to know in order to understand how C programs are written and what they do when they are run.

If you already have some programming experience in one or more other languages you may be tempted to skip over some of the introductory sections. That's fine. But don't be too eager to skip over too much. While C has quite a bit in common with some other languages, such as Java, that have adopted a 'C-like' syntax, it also has a great many important differences. For example, C is not object oriented, it has no string data type and it is much 'lower level' (closer to the way the computer hardware actually works) than many other languages. As a consequence, it doesn't offer as much protection from many common errors.

Do you need to read everything?

If you are fairly new to programming, you will get the most from this book by reading every chapter in order. If you are a more experienced programmer, feel free to jump into whichever chapters are of most interest to you. The example programs are all short and self-contained so you don't need to study the book in strict order.

In this book, I will highlight many of the problems that novice C programmers tend to make – everything from 'buffer overruns' to memory leaks. I'll also explain the special features of C such as its operators, typedefs, header files and loops.

The source code of all the examples is supplied in the code archive which you should download from the Bitwise Books web site. I strongly recommend that you compile and run the sample programs using your C compiler. Better still, use a C IDE with a debugger to step through the code one line at a time in order to understand it better. Some popular C compilers and IDEs are listed in the Appendix.

Unsafe Functions

Occasionally, in the source code examples, you may find that I have used an 'old-style' C function which your compiler may warn you is 'unsafe'. If your compiler recommends an alternative function, by all means use it. Not all compilers support the same alternative functions, however. So, for the sake of compatibility, my code samples will often use 'traditional', widely-supported but sometimes outdated functions such as strcat(). For more on unsafe functions, refer to the Appendix.

The Visual Studio Projects

All the code in the archive is provided as a single Visual Studio solution that can be loaded direct into Microsoft's Visual Studio IDE (see the Appendix for more information). In the Visual Studio solution I have defined (in a 'property sheet') which includes a pre-processor definition of `_CRT_SECURE_NO_WARNINGS` to silence error messages associated with some old ('unsafe') C functions. If you are writing your own code you may need to include this line at the start of the file to do the same thing.

```
#define _CRT_SECURE_NO_WARNINGS
```

Using the Code With Other IDEs

The code in the source code archive may be edited and compiled using a variety of different C editors, IDEs and tools in addition to Visual Studio. The Appendix contains more information. We also have some free downloads on the Bitwise Books web site which provide additional help on using some other popular IDEs for programming C.

2 – First Programs

Once you have installed a C compiler and a C source code editor you are ready to start programming in C. In this chapter you will write, compile and run your first C programs.

Without more ado, let's start writing some C code. This is the traditional "Hello World" program in C:

HelloWorld

```
#include <stdio.h>

main() {
    printf("hello world\n");
}
```

This program uses (that is, it 'includes') code from the C 'standard input/output library, `stdio`, using this statement:

```
#include <stdio.h>
```

What is a header?

You will often see in the C example programs, right at the start of the file, something like this:

```
#include <stdio.h>
```

This is an instruction to the C compiler to 'include' the file '*stdio.h*' directly into your program. This is called a 'header' file. A header file contains (among other things) definitions of the various functions we need to use so that the compiler knows what to do when it comes across one of them. I discuss header files in more detail in Chapter 8.

The code that starts with the name `main` is the 'main function' – in other words, it is the first bit of code that runs when the program runs. The function name is followed by a pair of parentheses. The code to be run is enclosed between a pair of curly brackets:

```
main() {
}
```

Functions

A function is a named block of code. We look at functions in detail in Chapter 5. In C, the `main()` function runs automatically when your program starts.

In the *HelloWorld* program, the code calls the `printf()` function – a function that is provided as standard by C – to print the string (the piece of text) between double-quotes. When we talk about 'printing' a string, we usually don't mean that the string is printed on paper using a printer. We mean that it is 'printed' to the output which is another way of saying that it is displayed on screen. The `"\n"` at the end of the string causes a new line to be displayed:

```
printf("hello world\n");
```

The Anatomy of a C Program

Every C program is made up of elements such as keywords, functions and variables. In this section we'll quickly summarize the main elements of a C program. Finally we'll see how some of these elements are used in the "Hello World" program.

The C Language

If you are new to programming or are unfamiliar with the syntax of C, you may want to refer to the Appendix, *'Elements of the C Language'* which contains some simple definitions of some of the most important features of C.

Hello World Revisited

Let's take a closer look at the simple "Hello world" program that this chapter began with and try to identify the various elements of C code.

```
#include[1] <stdio.h>[2]

main[3]()[4] {[5]
    printf[6]("hello world\n"[7]);[8]
}
```

1. `#include` is a pre-processor directive. Here it causes the contents of the file *stdio.h* to be included in the current program.
2. The pointy brackets, `< >`, around the file name tell the compiler to search for that file (here the 'header' file *stdio.h*) in the 'C system' directories.
3. `main` is the name of the function that is run when the program starts.
4. The empty pair of parentheses after `main` show that this is a function with no arguments.
5. The curly braces `{` and `}` delimit code blocks. Here they enclose the code of the `main` function.
6. `printf()` is a function defined in the file *stdio.h*.
7. `"hello world\n"` is a string of characters, passed between the parentheses to the `printf()` function; `"\n"` is the 'newline' character.
8. The semicolon terminates the statement.

The "Hello world" program could be rewritten like this:

HelloWorldAgain

```
#include <stdio.h>

int main(int argc, char **argv) {
    printf("hello world\n");
    return 0;
}
```

In fact, if you create a new C project using some programming environments, code similar to the above will be generated automatically. When this program is run, you will see no difference from the last program – it too displays "Hello world" followed by a newline.

The main differences are that this time the name of the `main()` function is preceded by `int`. This shows that the function returns an integer (a whole number) when it finishes running. The number 0 is returned in the last line of the function:

```
return 0;
```

This return value is unlikely to be of any significance in your programs and, for the time being at any rate, you can ignore it. By tradition, a value of 0 just means that the program ran without any errors. Any other value might indicate an 'error code'.

The other difference is that this program contains two 'arguments', called `argc` and `argv`, between parentheses:

```
int main(int argc, char **argv)
```

These arguments may optionally be initialized with values passed to the program when it is run. I'll show an example of this in the next sample program.

******

The two asterisks before `argv` are important:

```
char **argv
```

They indicate that `argv` is a list of strings. Strictly speaking `argv` is an 'argument vector' or a pointer to an array (a sequential list) of strings, where each string is itself an array of characters. It's not important to understand this for now. We look at arrays and pointers in Chapter 7.

To pass values to the program, you can just run the program at the command prompt and put any arguments (items of data – numbers or words) after the name of the program itself, with spaces between each item.

For example, if I wanted to pass the arguments "hello" and "world" to the program *HelloWorldArgs.exe* (on Windows) or *HelloWorldArgs.app* (on a Mac) I would enter this at the command prompt or terminal:

```
HelloWorldArgs hello world
```

My program 'receives' those two bits of data and it stores them in the second argument, `argv`. The first argument, `argc` is an automatically calculated value that represents the total number of the arguments stored in `argv`.

This is the program code:

HelloWorldArgs

```
int main(int argc, char **argv) {
int i;

for (i = 0; i < argc; i++) {
        printf("Hello World! argc=%d arg %d is %s\n", argc, i, argv[i]);
    }
    return 0;
}
```

When I pass the program the two arguments: `hello` and `world`, this is the output which is displayed:

```
Hello World! argc=3 arg 0 is HelloWorldArgs
Hello World! argc=3 arg 1 is hello
Hello World! argc=3 arg 2 is world
```

This shows that the count (`argc`) of arguments is 3 even though I have only passed two arguments. That's because the program name itself, `HelloWorldArgs`, is automatically passed as the first argument. The first argument here has the index number 0. The arguments at index 1 and 2 are the arguments that I passed to the program: `hello` and `world`.

The block of code that starts with the keyword `for` is a loop that causes the code that follows it, between the curly braces, to execute for a certain number of times. Here the code executes for the number of times indicated by the value of the `argc` argument. The `printf` statement prints the string `"Hello World! argc=%d arg %d is %s\n"` and it substitutes the values of `argc`, `i`, `argv[i]`, at the points marked by `%d`, `%d` and `%s` in the string. At each turn through the `for` loop the string at the index `i` in the `argv` array is printed.

for Loops

`for` loops are very commonly used in C so we need to get to grips with the syntax right away. Here is a simple example of a `for` loop:

```
int i;
for (i = 1; i < 100; i++) {
    dosomething();
}
```

The code between the parentheses after the word `for` controls the loop execution:

```
for (i = 1; i < 100; i++)
```

This code is divided into three parts:

`i = 1`	Initialise an `int` variable, `i`, with the value 1.
`i < 100`	Test if `i` is less than 100. The loop runs while this test is true.
`i++`	Increment (add 1 to) the value of `i` at each turn through the loop.

We could paraphrase the code of the `for` loop shown above like this:

- Set the value of `i` to 1.
- While i is less than 100 run the code inside the loop.
- Then add 1 to i.

Note that this loop will execute 99 times, not 100, since it will fail when the value of `i` is no longer less than 100.

++

The `++` operator adds 1 to the value of an integer variable. This sort of operator will be explained in Chapter 4.

puts and printf

There are several functions that can be used to display (print) information when your C programs run. Both `printf()` and `puts()`, can display a simple string.

```
printf("hello world\n");
puts("hello world again");
```

puts

The `puts()` function automatically appends a newline character to the end of the string; the `printf()` function does not, so I have had to add a newline character by putting `'\n'` at the end of the string displayed by `printf()`. The newline character causes the text to skip onto a new line when the program runs.

printf

The `printf()` function is more generally useful than `puts()` because also allows you to embed 'format specifiers' into a string. A format specifier begins with a `%` and is followed by a letter: `%s` specifies a string, `%d` specifies a decimal or integer.

When format specifiers occur in the string, the string must be followed by a comma-delimited list of values. These values replace the specifiers embedded into the string. The programmer must take care that the values in the list exactly match the types and the number of the format specifiers in the string otherwise the program may crash. Here is an example:

printf

```
int main(int argc, char **argv) {
    printf("hello world\n");
    puts("hello world again");
    printf("There are %d bottles standing on the %s.\n", 20, "wall");
    return 0;
}
```

When run, the code produces the following output:

```
hello world
hello world again
There are 20 bottles standing on the wall.

```

Notice the final blank line in the output shown above. That's not a mistake. When the program runs, the text-entry cursor ends up on a new, blank line because the last `printf()` ends with a newline character `'\n'`.

3 – Variables, Types and Constants

In the last chapter, I gave a very brief explanation of variables and types. These are fundamental in C programming. In this chapter we'll be looking at them in more detail.

A variable is like the programming equivalent of a labelled box. You might have a box labelled 'Petty Cash' or a variable named `pettycash`. Just as the contents of the box might vary (as money is put into it and taken out again), so the contents of a variable might change as new values are assigned to it. You assign a value using the equals sign (`=`).

Variables and Types

In C a variable is declared by stating its data-type (such as `int` for an integer variable or `double` for a 'double precision' floating-point variable) followed by the variable name. You can invent names for your variables and, as a general rule, it is best to make those names descriptive.

This is how to declare a floating-point variable with the `double` data-type. Here I have named the variable `mydouble`:

```
double mydouble;
```

You can now assign a floating-point value to that variable:

```
mydouble = 100.75;
```

Alternatively, you can assign a value at the same time you declare the variable:

```
double mydouble = 100.75;
```

Floating-point Numbers

There are several data types which can be used when declaring floating point variables in C. The `float` type represents single-precision numbers; `double` represents double-precision numbers and `long double` represents higher precision numbers. Higher precision types can store bigger values with greater precision. In this book, I shall normally use `double` for floating-point variables.

Variable names

A variable is simply a name or 'identifier' to which some value can be assigned. A variable name can include alphabetic characters, numbers and underscores but the first character of the name cannot be a number. So `xxx`, `a22` and `a_bc` can all be used as variable names but `22a` cannot.

Integers and Floats

Let's look at a program that uses both integer and floating point variables to do a calculation. My intention is to calculate the grand total of an item by starting with its subtotal (its value without tax) and then calculating the amount of tax due on it by multiplying that subtotal by the current tax rate.

Here I'm assuming the tax rate to be 17.5% or, expressed as a floating point number, 0.175. I calculate the final price by adding the calculated tax into the grand total:

01 Calc

```
#include <stdio.h>

int main(int argc, char **argv) {
    int subtotal;
    int tax;
    int grandtotal;
    double taxrate;

    taxrate = 0.175;
    subtotal = 250;
    tax = subtotal * taxrate;
    grandtotal = subtotal + tax;
    printf("The tax on %d is %d, so the grand total is %d.\n",
                subtotal, tax, grandtotal);
    return 0;
}
```

Once again, I use the `printf()` function to display the results. Remember that the three place-markers, `%d`, are replaced by the values of the three matching variables: `subtotal`, `tax` and `grandtotal`.

When you run the program, this is what you will see:

```
The tax on 250 is 43, so the grand total is 293.
```

But there is a problem here. If you can't see what it is, try doing the same calculation using a calculator. If you calculate the tax, 250 * 0.175, the result you get should be 43.75 which is closer to 44 than to 43. Even so, 43 is the result that is shown by my program.

This is due to the fact that I have calculated using a floating-point number (the `double` variable, `taxrate`) but I have assigned the result to an integer number (the `int` variable, `tax`). An integer variable can only represent numbers with no fractional part so any values after the floating point are ignored. That has introduced an error into the code.

The error is easy to fix. I just need to use floating-point variables instead of integer variables. Here is my rewritten code:

02 Calc

```
#include <stdio.h>

int main(int argc, char **argv) {
    double subtotal;
    double tax;
    double grandtotal;
    double taxrate;

    taxrate = 0.175;
    subtotal = 250;
    tax = subtotal * taxrate;
    grandtotal = subtotal + tax;
    printf("The tax on %.2f is %.2f, so the grand total is %.2f.\n",
            subtotal, tax, grandtotal);
    return 0;
}
```

This time all the variables are doubles so their values are not truncated. This is now the output:

```
The tax on 250.00 is 43.75, so the grand total is 293.75.
```

I have also used the float `%f` specifiers to display the float values in the string which I have passed to the `printf()` function. In fact, you will see that the format specifiers in the string also include a dot and a number numbers like this: `%.2f`. This tells `printf()` to display at least two digits to the right of the decimal point.

You can also format a number by specifying its width – that is, the minimum number of characters it should occupy in the string. So if I were to write `%4.2f` that would tell `printf()` to format the number in a space that takes up at least 4 characters with two digits to the right of the decimal point. Try entering different numbers in the format specifiers (e.g. `%10.4f`) to see the effects these numbers have.

Numeric format specifiers

Here are examples of numeric formatting specifiers to use with `printf()`:

`%d`	print as decimal integer
`%4d`	print as decimal integer, at least 4 characters wide
`%f`	print as floating point
`%4f`	print as floating point, at least 4 characters wide
`%.2f`	print as floating point, 2 characters after decimal point
`%4.2f`	print as floating point, at least 4 wide and 2 after decimal point

Constants

If you want to make sure that a value cannot be changed, you should declare a constant. A constant is an identifier to which a value is assigned but whose value (unlike the value of a variable) should never change during the execution of your program.

#define

The traditional way of defining a constant is C is to use the pre-processor directive `#define` followed by an identifier and a value to be substituted for that identifier. Here, for example, is how I might define a constant named `PI` with the value 3.141593:

```
#define PI 3.141593
```

In fact, the value of a constant defined in this way is not absolutely guaranteed to be immune from being changed by having a different value associated with the identifier.

In C, the following code is legal (though your compiler may show a warning message):

```
#define PI 3.141593
#define PI 55.5
```

How does #define work?

`#define` is a directive to the C pre-processor – a tool that processes source code before it is compiled into machine code. You may place an identifier (such as `PI`) after `#define` and then some characters (such as `3.141593`). The pre-processor replaces the identifier with the specified characters. If I define `PI` to be `3.141593`, whenever I now write `PI` in my code, the value `3.141593` is substituted before the program is compiled.

const

Modern C compilers provide an alternative way of defining constants using the keyword `const`, like this:

```
const double PI = 3.141593;
```

If I try to assign a new value to this type of constant the compiler won't let me. It shows an error message, so this is not permitted:

```
const double PI = 3.141593;
const double PI = 55.5;
```

In the sample program, *03_Calc* (see the listing on the next page), I have shown three alternative versions of my tax calculator. If you want to understand the difference between `#define` and `const`, try out that code.

This is the code of the *03_Calc* program from the source code archive:

03 Calc

```
#include <stdio.h>

int main(int argc, char **argv) {
#define TAXRATE_DEFINED 0.175
    const double TAXRATE_CONST = 0.175;

    double subtotal;
    double tax;
    double grandtotal;
    double taxrate;

    taxrate = 0.175;
    subtotal = 200;
    taxrate = 0.2;                   // redefine a variable
    tax = subtotal * taxrate;
    grandtotal = subtotal + tax;

    printf("(taxrate is %.3f) The tax on %.2f is %.2f, so the grand total\
 is %.2f.\n",
        taxrate, subtotal,tax, grandtotal);

    subtotal = 200;
#define TAXRATE_DEFINED 0.2            // redefine a #define
    tax = subtotal * TAXRATE_DEFINED;
    grandtotal = subtotal + tax;

    printf("(TAXRATE_DEFINED is %.3f) The tax on %.2f is %.2f, so the grand
total\
 is %.2f.\n",
            TAXRATE_DEFINED, subtotal, tax, grandtotal);
    subtotal = 200;
    // TAXRATE_CONST = 0.2;           // cannot redefine const!
    tax = subtotal * TAXRATE_CONST;
    grandtotal = subtotal + tax;

    printf("(TAXRATE_CONST is %.3f) The tax on %.2f is %.2f, so the grand total\
is %.2f.\n",
                TAXRATE_CONST, subtotal, tax, grandtotal);
    return 0;
}
```

Comments

You may have notices some explanatory text embedded into the code of the *03_Calc* sample program, like this:

```
taxrate = 0.2;                  // redefine a variable
```

Here the text following the // characters is a comment. Comments are used to document code. They ignored by the compiler. Comments following // extend to the end of a single line. If you want to have comments that extend over multiple-lines, you can place them between /* and */ like this:

```
/* This comment runs over three
   lines. It can be used to document
   code and is ignored by the compiler. */
```

Sometimes, when you want to test code or fix an error, you may 'comment out' a line. I had to do that with the line that tried to redefine a `const` because the compiler would not compile it:

```
// TAXRATE_CONST = 0.2;
```

There are explanations of comments and other fundamental features of the C language in the Appendix: *Elements of the C Language*.

Variable, #define or const?

First I use the variable `taxrate` to store the tax rate to be used in calculations:

```
double taxrate;
taxrate = 0.175;
```

Then I `#define` constant `TAXRATE_DEFINED`:

```
#define TAXRATE_DEFINED 0.175
```

And, finally, I declare the `const` constant, `TAXRATE_CONST`:

```
const double TAXRATE_CONST = 0.175;
```

So, in principle, I now have three identifiers that store the value 0.175: a variable, a `#defined` symbol and a constant. So what is the difference?

Well, naturally, the value of the variable can be reassigned. That's what a variable is for. But in this case I specifically want to guarantee that the tax rate *cannot* be changed. Many C programmers would therefore prefer a `#defined` symbol which would be treated as a constant. But, in fact, treating `#defined` symbols as constants is just a programming *convention*. The C pre-processor and compiler don't respect that convention and if you go ahead and redefine the value of the symbol, it will be allowed. So, this is permitted:

```
#define TAXRATE_DEFINED 0.175
#define TAXRATE_DEFINED 0.2
```

But it is not permitted to redefine the value of a true constant (declared using the `const` keyword). This code will *not* compile:

```
const double TAXRATE_CONST = 0.175;
TAXRATE_CONST = 0.2;
```

Naming Conventions

You may have noticed that I have named my constants (both those declared using `const` and those declared using `#define`) in capital letters like this:

```
TAXRATE_CONST, TAXRATE_DEFINED, PI.
```

Naming constants using all capital letters with the individual 'words' separated by underscores is a widely adopted convention in C. Bear in mind, however, that it is only a convention and not a rule.

When you write C code you may want to adopt some other conventions when writing the names of variables and functions. These are some common conventions:

Lowercase for variable names:

```
int tax;
```

Lowercase for function names:

```
int calculate() {
}
```

Lowercase for parameter names (named arguments between parentheses):

```
int calculate_grand_total(int subtotal)
```

Underscores to separate 'words' in function and variable names:

```
int calculate_grand_total(int subtotal) {
    int grand_total;

    grand_total = subtotal + SERVICE_CHARGE;
    return grand_total;
}
```

Once again, let me emphasise that these are only conventions. You are not obliged to name your functions and variables in this way. In fact, some programmers adopt other conventions.

For example, many people prefer to use mixed-case letters to divide 'words' instead of underscores, like this:

```
int calculateGrandTotal(int subTotal) {
    int grandTotal;

    grandTotal = subTotal + ServiceCharge;
    return grandTotal;
}
```

Whichever naming convention you choose, try to be consistent. In this book, I will generally use lowercase letters separated by underscores for the names of functions, uppercase letters for constants, and lowercase or mixed-case letters for parameters and variables. But that is just my choice and other programmers will adopt other naming conventions.

Case sensitivity

Be aware that C is a case-sensitive language, so a variable called `subtotal` is treated as a different variable from one called `subTotal` or one called `subTOTAL`. Similarly, a function that is named `my_function()` is different from one named `my_Function()` or `My_Function()`.

Meaningful Names

Another important point when naming variables and functions is to choose names that describe what those variables and functions actually do. Look at this code:

```
#define v 33

int myfunc(int z) {
    int t;

    t = z + v;
    return t;
}
```

It tells you nothing at all about what the function is intended to do. Below I have rewritten this function. The two versions of this function (the one above and the one below) do exactly the same operations. However, I think you will agree that this rewritten version of the function is much easier to make sense of!

```
#define SERVICE_CHARGE 33

int calculate_grand_total(int subtotal) {
    int grand_total;

    grand_total = subtotal + SERVICE_CHARGE;
    return grand_total;
}
```

Hmmm, what does *that* mean?

Often a piece of code will make perfect sense at the time you write it. But then, when you revisit that code at some future date, it may make no sense at all – because you have forgotten what your original intentions were when you wrote it. Remember that the time spent making your code *absolutely* clear is time well spent.

The code in the *NamingConventions* project shows a mix of naming conventions. For example, one `#define` identifier is all lowercase, another uses underscores, a third is uppercase. This can be confusing. It is generally better to adopt a consistent naming convention.

Pay attention to the fact `do_something()` and `Do_Something()` are treated as different functions. This is due to C's case sensitivity.

NamingConventions

```
#include <stdio.h>

#define somevalue 10
#define some_other_value 15
#define SERVICE_CHARGE 33

int do_something(int x) {
    return x + somevalue;
}

int Do_Something(int x) {
    return x + some_other_value;
}

int calculate_grand_total(int subtotal) {
    int grand_total;

    grand_total = subtotal + SERVICE_CHARGE;
    return grand_total;
}

int main(int argc, char **argv) {
    printf("%d\n", do_something(500));
    printf("%d\n", Do_Something(600));
    printf("%d\n", calculate_grand_total(700));
    return 0;
}
```

Code formatting

Different programmers have different ideas about what counts as 'good' source code formatting. Some people like to put every opening curly bracket onto its own new line. Others (like me!) prefer to save screen-space by putting the opening curly bracket on the same line as the code (such as the function header) which precedes it. Some people like to put a space after every opening parenthesis and before every closing parenthesis. I prefer not to. Many IDEs (such as Visual Studio) provide automatic code formatting options so that you can try to be consistent with spaces, newlines, indentation and so on. One formatting preference you will notice in my code is to declare all variables at the start of the functions in which they occur and place a blank line after them. This is purely for the sake of clarity.

4 – Tests, Operators and Input

In your programs you will often want to assign values to variables and, later on, test those values. For example, you might write a program in which you test the age of an employee in order to calculate his or her bonus. In order to do that you need to understand how to use some C operators and take different actions based on the results of tests.

Here I use the 'greater than' operator > to test if the value of the `age` variable is greater than 45:

```
if (age > 45) {
    bonus = 1000;
}
```

What is an operator?

An operator is a special symbol which tells the compiler to perform a simple mathematical or logical function, to perform a comparison or assign a value.

We've already used operators such as the addition operator `+`, the multiplication operator `*` and the assignment operator `=` in code like this (from Chapter 3):

```
tax = subtotal * TAXRATE_DEFINED;
grandtotal = subtotal + tax;
```

The time has come to look at C's operators in a bit more detail.

The Assignment Operator

One of the most important operators is = which is the assignment operator. This assigns the value on its right to a variable on its left. Note that the type of data assigned must be compatible with the type of the variable.

This is an assignment of an integer (10) to an `int` variable named `myintvariable`:

```
int myintvariable;
myintvariable = 10;
```

Assignment or equality?

Beware. *One* equals sign = is used to assign a value (it gives to a variable on its left the value on its right). But *two* equals signs == are used to test a condition.

= This is the *assignment* operator.

```
x = 1;
```

The variable x now has the value 1.

== This is the *equality* operator.

```
if (x == 1)
```

If the value of x is 1, this test evaluates to *true*. If it is any other value it evaluates to *false*.

Tests and Comparisons

C can perform tests using the `if` statement. The test itself must be contained within parentheses and it should be capable of evaluating to true or false. If true, the statement following the test executes. Optionally, an `else` clause may follow the `if` clause and this will execute if the test evaluates to false. Here is an example:

Operators

```
if (age > 45) {
    bonus = 1000;
} else {
    bonus = 500;
}
```

You may use other operators to perform other tests. For example, the code below tests if the value of `age` is less than or equal to 70. If it is, then the test evaluates to true and "You are one of our youngest employees!" is displayed. Otherwise the condition evaluates to false and nothing is displayed:

```
if (age <= 70){
    printf("You are one of our youngest employees!\n");
}
```

Notice that the `<=` operator means 'less than *or* equal to'. It performs a different test than the `<` operator which means 'less than'. In the sample project, the value of `age` is 70. Edit the test to use the `<` operator like this and run the program again to understand the difference:

```
if (age < 70)
```

Comparison operators

These are the most common comparison operators that you will use in tests:

`==`	equals
`!=`	not equals
`>`	greater than
`<`	less than
`<=`	less than or equal to
`>=`	greater than or equal to

Compound Assignment Operators

Some assignment operators in C perform a calculation prior to assigning the result to a variable. This table shows some examples of common 'compound assignment operators' along with the non-compound equivalent.

Operator	Example	Equivalent to
`+=`	`a += b`	`a = a + b`
`-=`	`a -= b`	`a = a - b`
`*=`	`a *= b`	`a = a * b`
`/=`	`a /= b`	`a = a / b`

It is up to you which syntax you prefer to use in your own code. Many C programmers prefer compound operators as in: `a += b`.

But the same effect is achieved using the slightly longer form as in: `a = a + b`.

Increment ++ and Decrement -- Operators

When you want to increment or decrement by 1 (that is, add 1 to, or subtract 1 from) the value of a variable, you may also use the `++` and `--` operators. Here is an example of the increment (`++`) operator:

```
int a;
a = 10;
a++;      // a is now 11
```

This is an example of the decrement (`--`) operator:

```
int a;
a = 10;
a--;      // a is now 9
```

Why so many operators?

Given the fact that you can add or subtract 1 from a variable like this:

```
x = x + 1;
x = x - 1;
```

Or like this:

```
x += 1;
x -= 1;
```

Why does C also have the `++` and `--` operators? The simple answer is because incrementing values by 1 is such a common operation that it is very slightly quicker to enter these operators into your code like this:

```
x++;
x--;
```

C is known for its 'terse' or 'concise' syntax. These operators are an extreme example of this.

Prefix and Postfix Operators

You may place the `++` and `--` operators either before or after a variable like this: `a++` or like this: `++a`. When placed before a variable (prefix), the value is incremented *before* any assignment is made:

```
num1 = 10;
num2 = ++num1;              // num2 = 11, num1 = 11
```

When placed after a variable (postfix), the assignment of the *existing* value is done *before* the variable's value is incremented:

```
num1 = 10;
num2 = num1++;              // num2 = 10, num1 = 11
```

As a general rule, I would recommend that you stick to using `++` and `--` as postfix operators. In fact, there is often nothing wrong with using the longer form `a = a + 1` or `a = a - 1`. Mixing prefix and postfix operators in your code can be confusing and may lead to hard-to-find bugs. So, whenever possible, keep it simple and keep it clear.

if...else

At the start of the chapter, I gave an example of testing a condition using `if`, like this:

```
if (age > 45)
```

In that example, the value of `age` (70) was assigned in my code and so it was bound to be the same value every time the program was run. In a real-world program, that would not be very useful.

In the *TestAge1* project (shown on the next page), I have created a simple program that prompts the user to enter their age so the value of the `age` variable may be different each time the program runs.

TestAge1

```
int main(int argc, char **argv) {
    char agestring[10];
    int age;
    int bonus;

    printf("Enter your age : ");
    gets(agestring);
    age = atoi(agestring);
    if (age > 45) {
        bonus = 1000;
    } else {
        bonus = 500;
    }
    printf("Your age is %d, so your bonus is %d.\n", age, bonus);
    return(0);
}
```

In order to get input from the command prompt I have used the `gets()` function. This obtains the text that was entered at the prompt. It assigns this text to the variable between parentheses. This variable is treated as a string (that is, a series – or array – of alphanumeric characters). In this case, my variable, `agestring`, has been declared as an array of 10 characters:

```
char agestring[10];
```

But my `if` test requires an integer variable. I convert the string `agestring` to an integer using the `atoi()` function and I assign the result to the `int` variable named `age`:

```
age = atoi(agestring);
```

Once that is done, the value of `age` can be tested against an integer value:

```
if (age > 45) {
    bonus = 1000;
} else {
    bonus = 500;
}
```

But there is a problem here. What if the user enters some text that cannot be converted to an integer? Say, for example, when prompted to enter an age, the user enters the string "Forty"? The `atoi()` function can only convert a string that contains numerical characters such as "40".

When it tries to convert anything else it fails and it returns the value 0. In my program, a return value of 0 is treated as a valid age, a bonus will be applied and this message will be displayed:

```
Your age is 0, so your bonus is 500.
```

That is clearly not what I intended. So how do I fix this problem?

atoi() potential problems

`atoi()` will also work with values that commence with a number and end with other non-numeric characters such as "123xyz". It silently ignores the "xyz" when converting the numeric part of the string. `atoi()` is an old function which I use here because it has a very simple syntax, it is provided by a large number of compilers and is used in many standard C programming texts. Modern C compilers provide alternative conversion functions such as `strtol()`, `atoi_l()` and others. Search your compiler's documentation to see which conversion routines it recommends.

One simple solution to the problem is to test if the value of is age 0 and take specific action if it is (for example, display an error message) and only if it is not 0 continue to perform the regular test. I have done this in *TestAge2*. This illustrates how to 'nest' `if` and `else` tests:

TestAge2

```
if (age == 0) {                         // if #1...
    printf("You entered an invalid age, so your bonus cannot be calculated.\n");
} else {                                         // ...else #1
    if (age > 45) {                     // if #2...
        bonus = 1000;
    } else {                                     // ...else #2
        bonus = 500;
    }
    printf("Your age is %ds, so your bonus is %d.\n", age, bonus);
}
```

Here, I test if the value of `age` is 0. If it is this message is displayed: "You entered an invalid age, so your bonus cannot be calculated.\n". If `age` has any other value then the code block following the first `else` executes.

This block contains all the code between the outermost set of curly brackets:

```
else {
    if (age > 45) {
        bonus = 1000;
    } else {
        bonus = 500;
    }
    printf("Your age is %ds, so your bonus is %d.\n", age, bonus);
}
```

This code includes another `if...else` test. Remember that this second `if...else` test only executes when the first `if` test fails (if `age` was not 0).

Nested if...else tests

Nested `if...else` tests (that is, `if...else` tests that are placed within code blocks that are controlled by other `if...else` tests) are not uncommon in C programs. However, don't overdo them. If you have `if...else` tests that are nested more than one-level deep, the logic of the tests may be hard to understand. If you find you've written code with many nested levels of `if` or `if...else` tests, consider rewriting the code to make it easier to understand.

gets() and fgets()

The last program may *seem* to work as expected. However, there is a potential problem. It turns out that the `gets()` function will go ahead and assign any amount of text that the user happens to enter at the command prompt to the variable specified.

Recall that I defined the `agestring` variable to have a maximum of 10 characters:

```
char agestring[10];
```

What happens, then, if the user enters 20 or 25 characters? To clarify this problem, try out the *GetInput* program.

gets()

Look at the function named getinput_with_gets():

GetInput

```
void getinput_with_gets() {
    char firstname[5];
    char lastname[5];

    printf("Enter your first name:");
    gets(firstname);
    printf("Enter your last name:");
    gets(lastname);
    printf("Hello, %s, %s\n", firstname, lastname);
}
```

Here gets() tries to read in all the characters that have been entered but it only assigns a fixed number (5) of those characters to the fixed-length array, firstname. That's fine if I only enter 4 characters (the 5th character will be the carriage return). But if I enter more than 4 characters then I will have a problem. That's because the data that I enter spills over the end of the memory used by the 5-character array that was declared to hold that data – and the overspilled characters will end up in some unpredictable area of my computer's memory.

The chances are that those extra characters will overwrite some bit of memory that is already being used for something else. At best, this means that the data which I assign to my variables may be incorrect (it may include some of the 'overspill' characters). At worst, it could mean that my program crashes. In fact, this behaviour was considered so undesirable that gets() was removed from the latest C11 standard, though it is available in earlier compilers. It is also still available in the C libraries since so many older programs used it. gets() illustrates one of the major problems with writing C code – it is very, very easy to unintentionally overwrite memory. For that reason, even though the gets() function may seem easy to use, I would not encourage you to do so in a finished program. Refer to the Appendix for more on this.

fgets()

The fgets() function is a safer alternative to gets(). The fgets() function takes three 'arguments' between parentheses:

1) the array to which the data will be assigned.
2) the maximum number of characters to be read.
3) the name of the data-source or 'stream' from which to read.

The data-source may be a file on disk. Alternatively, the name `stdin` indicates that the source is the 'standard input' – here, that means any text entered by the user. The value specified for the maximum number of characters causes a string to be truncated at the specified number *less one*.

Let's assume you use the value 5 as shown below:

```
fgets(firstname, 5, stdin);
```

If you now enter five characters at the command prompt like this: "abcde", only the first four characters, "abcd", will be read. That is because the fifth character is a special 'null' character (`'\0'`) which is automatically appended to a string.

Null terminated strings

Unlike many other programming languages, C doesn't have a string data-type. Instead it treats an array of characters ending with a null (a 0-value character) as a string. This will be explained in Chapter 7.

There is still one problem, however. If you enter more characters than are actually processed by your code, those characters remain in memory, waiting to be processed. So when you next try to read some characters from the command line, the characters waiting to be processed will be read in first.

Let's look at an example. Assume you have this code:

GetInput

```
void getinput_with_fgets() {
    char firstname[5];
    char lastname[5];

    printf("Enter your first name:");
    fgets(firstname, 5, stdin);
    printf("Enter your last name:");
    fgets(lastname, 5, stdin);
    printf("Hello, %s, %s\n", firstname, lastname);
}
```

When you enter "abcde" and press the enter key, the first 4 characters, "abcd", are assigned to the variable `firstname`. You probably now expect that you will be prompted to enter your last name. But that is not what happens.

What happens is that the two *unprocessed* characters (the `'e'` plus the carriage return `'\n'` that you entered previously) are immediately processed by the next `fgets()` and those two characters are assigned to the `lastname` variable. The final `printf()` then displays the following:

```
Hello, abcd, e
```

Flushing Buffers

In order to fix this we need to 'use up' the extra characters that were entered but were not assigned to the `firstname` variable. To use programming jargon, the spare characters are said to be stored in an array of characters called a 'buffer' and in order to use them up we need to empty or 'flush' that buffer.

What is a buffer?

A 'buffer' is an area of memory used for general purpose storage of data. Typically, a buffer is used for intermediate storage in input and output operations. The memory is said to 'buffer' the input and the output from the program code.

The simplest way to flush the buffer is to read through the remaining characters which it contains. In this case, I want to read all the characters up until a newline `'\n'` (which indicates the end of input entered at the command prompt). In fact, I also test for the end of a file (a negative integer value assigned to the `EOF` constant.

EOF

`EOF` (short for 'End Of File') is a symbol that is pre-defined in the file *stdio.h*, like this:

```
#define EOF    (-1)
```

Strictly speaking, it is not a constant (as explained in Chapter 3, a symbol defined using `#define` may be redefined). However, it is sometimes termed a 'symbolic constant'. It should be *treated* as a constant and you should never redefine it – as that could have a catastrophic effect on your programs!

This is my buffer-flushing function:

GetInput

```
void flush_input(){
    int ch;

    while ((ch = getchar()) != '\n' && ch != EOF);
}
```

The `!=` operator here means 'not equal to'. The `while` loop continues reading characters while the character that is read is not a newline character (`'\n'`) and (`&&`) it is also not at the end of a file (`EOF`). Here `&&` is one of C's logical operators which we will look at later in this chapter. I'll return to look at `while` loops more closely in Chapter 6.

fflush()

The standard C library function `fflush()` also flushes a buffer. However, it is defined to flush the *output* buffer (the characters being written) rather than the *input* buffer (the characters being read). *Some* implementations of `fflush()` work with both input and output but this cannot be relied upon across all C compilers and code libraries, which is why it may be safer to write your own input flushing routine.

There remains yet another problem with my code. The `fgets()` function reads in all the text entered including the newline `'\n'` character. That is not a problem if I enter more characters than will fit into my fixed-length arrays, `firstname` and `lastname`. In that case, the variables are initialized with the appropriate number of characters – and a null terminator is automatically appended by `fgets()`.

But if I enter fewer characters than are needed to initialize the variables, `fgets()` reads the newline character which was entered when I pressed the enter key. Then I call my `flush_input()` function. This carries on reading characters until a newline is found. But there is no longer a newline to be read because I have already processed that character. As a consequence I need to press the enter key a second time.

Keep It Simple!

I could rewrite the code to try to deal with this problem, but I'm already starting to find the code I've already written to be quite confusing. And when your code starts to be confusing, it's time to simplify it!

I've decided that I need a dedicated line-reading function to handle all the complexity. I want it to read a line of text up to a specified maximum length. I also want it to work in exactly the same way whether I enter a short bit of text, a long bit of text or even no text at all (should I just press the enter key). As an added extra it might be useful if it also returned the length of the text read, just in case I need to verify the length for some reason. That is what I have done in the *ReadLine* program.

A Custom Line Reading Function

Below is my first effort at writing a function which safely reads a line of text and assigns it to an array of characters (declared in the function header as `char s[]`).

What is char s[]?

Here `s` is the name of a parameter – which is a special sort of variable that can be assigned a piece of data (an 'argument') passed to a function. The square brackets after the parameter name show that it's an array, or sequential list, of data items. The type name `char` before the parameter name show that this is an array of characters. Functions and arguments are explained in more detail in Chapter 5. Arrays are the subject of Chapter 6. We look at the complexities of character arrays (strings) in Chapter 7.

ReadLine

```
int readln (char s[], int maxlen) {
    int len_s;

    fgets(s, maxlen, stdin);
    len_s = strlen(s);
    if (s[len_s - 1] == '\n') {
        s[len_s - 1] = '\0';
        len_s -= 1;
    }
    rewind(stdin); // This flushes the keyboard buffer
    return len_s;
}
```

- This function once again uses `fgets()` to get a string.
- The `maxlen` parameter specifies the maximum number of characters to read.
- I use the built-in function `strlen()` to get the length of the string.

The `if` block tests if the character at the end of the string (that is, at the position given by `len_s - 1`) is a newline character (`'\n'`) and, if it is, it replaces the newline character with a null character ('\0'). Remember that the null character is used in C to indicate the end of a string.

Finally I have used the rewind() function to flush the keyboard buffer instead of my own flush_input() function. It turns out that rewind() is used to move the focus back to the beginning of a file (technically, it repositions the file pointer to the beginning of a file). However, when stdin is passed to the function, rewind() has the effect of clearing the keyboard buffer.

Rewinding trouble

Using rewind() to flush the keyboard buffer looks like an easy solution. But there's a problem. It turns out that that the rewind() function is not the same on all operating systems. On Windows, for example, the input buffer is cleared, but in Linux it is not. With Linux, some other function such as tcflush() may be used instead.

Since not all buffer-flushing functions are the same with all C compilers on all operating systems, a case could be made for writing your own routine that does not rely upon any of the non-standard functions. That is what I have done in this alternative version of readln():

ReadLine

```
int readln(char s[], int maxlen) {
    char ch;
    int i;
    int chars_remain;
    i = 0;
    chars_remain = 1;
    while (chars_remain) {
        ch = getchar();
        if ((ch == '\n') || (ch == EOF)) {
            chars_remain = 0;
        } else if (i < maxlen - 1) {
            s[i] = ch;
            i++;
        }
    }
    s[i] = '\0';
    return i;
}
```

This reads the text entered at the keyboard one character at a time. All the reading is done using getchar() so I no longer have to worry about any side-effects due to newline characters that may, or may not, have been handled by the fgets() function.

Since my function now processes every character, it can not only assign the characters required to initialize variables but it can also process any extra characters in order to flush the keyboard buffer.

How Does readln() Work?

Let's take a close look at my `readln()` function. The code responsible for reading characters entered by the user has been put inside a `while` loop. This loop continues getting characters as long as any characters remain to be processed:

```
while (chars_remain) {
    ch = getchar();
    // ...more code here
}
```

I use an integer variable, `chars_remain`, to test whether the loop condition is true or false. This variable has the default value 1 (in C a non-zero value is regarded as meaning true when it is tested) and it becomes 0 (equivalent to false) when there are no more characters left.

True or False?

Many programming languages have dedicated True and False data types (Booleans). By tradition, C has a different way of representing True and False. A zero value integer is regarded as False. Any non-zero value is regarded as True. In fact, most modern implementations of C now also have Booleans (the `_Bool` type introduced in the C99 standard of the language). However, using integer values to represent True or False has become such an established tradition that it continues to be very widely used to this day.

Here the test evaluates to false when the newline character (or `EOF`) is found and so the `chars_remain` variable is assigned 0:

```
if ((ch == '\n') || (ch == EOF)) {
    chars_remain = 0;
```

A newline character will be found at the end of the input string – at the point at which I pressed the enter key. Until the newline character is found the `while` loop continues running.

At each turn through the loop the value of the counter variable is incremented (`i++`). The code fills the character array `s[]` by appending each character that has been read as long as `i` is less than `maxlen - 1` (here 1 is subtracted to allow for the terminating null character):

```
else if (i < maxlen - 1) {
    s[i] = ch;
```

The value of `maxlen` indicates the length of the character array that was passed to the `readln()` function. Once `i` is equal to or greater than `maxlen`, the code stops adding characters to `s[]`. However, that doesn't mean that the `while` loop stops running. Recall that this loop only stops running when a newline or `EOF` are found – and that might be either before or after I have finished adding characters to `s[]`.

If it is after `s[]` has been fully initialized then the reading of characters in the loop just serves the purpose of flushing the buffer – that is, it carries on reading and 'using up' any characters that I don't need.

Finally, I put a null character `'\0'` at the end of the `s[]` array. That marks the end of the string. And I return the value of `i` which gives the length of the string – not counting the terminating null character.

Writing and rewriting code

In this chapter I explain a number of problems I have found and handled when developing line-reading functions. Developers often write code in this way – by rewriting and refining their code to deal with problems as they arise. If you are new to programming you may find some of this section hard to understand at first reading. Don't worry. I will explain much of the technicality of this code – such as functions, arguments and null-terminated strings – in later chapters. For now just try to understand the process I've had to go through in identifying and solving a potential programming problem.

Logical Operators

In some of the code examples in this chapter, I have used the `&&` operator to mean 'and' and the `||` operator to mean 'or'. The `&&` and `||` operators are called 'logical operators'. Logical operators can help you chain together conditions when you want to take some action only when all of a set of conditions are true or when any one of a set of conditions is true.

For example, you might want to offer a discount to customers only when they have bought goods worth more than 100 dollars and they have *also* bought the deal of the day. In code these conditions could be evaluated using the logical *AND* (&&) operator, like this:

```
if ((valueOfPurchases > 100) && (boughtDealOfTheDay))
```

But if you are feeling more generous, you might want to offer a discount *either* if a customer has bought goods worth more than 100 dollars *OR* has bought the deal of the day. In C, these conditions can be evaluated using the logical *OR* (||) operator, like this:

```
if ((valueOfPurchases > 100) || (boughtDealOfTheDay))
```

Bitwise OR and logical OR

There is one other property of a logical operator that you should be aware of. Look at this code which uses || which is the logical *OR* operator:

```
if ((valueOfPurchases > 100) || (boughtDealOfTheDay))
```

If the first expression (`valueOfPurchases > 100`) is true then the second expression `boughtDealOfTheDay` will ***not*** be tested. Compare with the following code which uses | which is the bitwise *OR* operator:

```
if ((valueOfPurchases > 100) | (boughtDealOfTheDay))
```

Here, *both* expressions will ***always*** be used in the test. Logical operators are sometimes called 'short-circuit' operators – because they bypass ('short out') the second test when the first test evaluates to true (with ||) or false (with &&).

In contrast, bitwise operators, | and &, are typically used in constructing specific values of variables by setting, clearing or testing individual bits in a word. Bitwise operations are used for some advanced C programming tasks and won't be covered in detail in this book. Even so, you need to be clear on the different between the logical || operator and the bitwise | operator.

Boolean Values

Logical operators test Boolean values. A Boolean value can either be true or it can be false. As mentioned earlier, in C any non-zero value such as 1 or 100 is evaluated as true. A zero value is evaluated as false.

It is possible to create quite complex conditions by chaining together tests with multiple `&&` and `||` operators. But be careful. Complex tests are often hard to understand and if you make a mistake they may produce unwanted side effects. In addition, just as when you are using arithmetic operators, you may avoid ambiguity by grouping the individual 'test conditions' between parentheses.

The *LogicalOperators* sample program provides more examples of using logical operators.

LogicalOperators

```
#include <stdio.h>

int main(int argc, char **argv) {
    int age;
    int number_of_children;
    double salary;

    age = 25;
    number_of_children = 1;
    salary = 20000.00;

    if ((age <= 30) && (salary >= 30000)) {
        printf("You are a rich young person\n");
    } else {
        printf("You are not a rich young person\n");
    }

    if ((age <= 30) || (salary >= 30000)) {
        printf("You are either rich or young or     both\n");
    } else {
        printf("You are neither rich nor young\n");
    }

    if ((age <= 30) && (salary >= 30000) && (number_of_children != 0)) {
        printf("You are a rich young parent\n");
    } else {
        printf("You are not a rich young parent\n");
    }

    return 0;
}
```

The ! Operator

Note that the `!` operator can be used to negate a condition. So the test `!(a == b)` ('not a equals b') is equivalent to `(a != b)` ('a is not equal to b'). Similarly this test ...

```
(number_of_children != 0)
```

... could be rewritten like this:

```
!(number_of_children == 0)
```

switch

Up to now, when I've wanted to do a test of some sort I've used `if` and `else` statements. But if you need to do multiple `if...else` tests it is sometimes easier, and neater, to use 'switch' statements instead.

In C a `switch` statement begins with the keyword `switch` followed by a test value. This test value must be an integer or some piece of data (such as a `char`) that may be treated as an integer. For example, if I were testing the value of the `char` variable, `c`, I would write this:

```
switch (c)
```

This is followed by a pair of curly brackets containing one or more `case` statements, each of which specifies a value that is compared with the test value. If a match is made (when the `case` value and the test value are the same), the code following the `case` value and a colon executes. This is how I would test if the value of `c` is the char `'0'`. If it is, then my code sets the `chartype` variable to the string "Number":

SwitchCase

```
switch (c) {
    case '0':
        chartype = "Number";
        break;
}
```

When you want to exit the code in a `case` block you need to use the keyword `break`. If `case` tests are not followed by `break`, sequential `case` tests will be done one after the other until `break` is encountered. In this code, if `c` matches any of the characters from `'0'` to `'9'` the code after `case '9':` runs and `chartype` is set to "Number":

SwitchCase (continued)

```
switch (c) {
    case '0':
    case '1':
    case '2':
    case '3':
    case '4':
    case '5':
    case '6':
    case '7':
    case '8':
    case '9':
        chartype = "Number";
        break;
}
```

Falling Through the case Statement

When no match is made on one `case` test, the flow of execution continues through all other tests until a `break` is met. When writing long and complicated `switch` statements it is quite easy to forget to put a `break` after every test. This is called 'falling through' a `case` statement and, when unintentional, it can easily introduce a bug into your program.

ASCII codes and characters

The acronym, ASCII, stands for American Standard Code for Information Interchange. The alphabetic and numeric characters displayed on your screen may be represented internally by a specific code number in the ASCII table. For example, ASCII code 66 equates to the upper-case 'A' character, whereas ASCII code 97 equates to a lower-case 'a'. There are also ASCII codes for invisible characters such as spaces (ASCII 32) and Carriage Returns (ASCII 13). There is even a backspace character (ASCII 8) which is generated by the backspace key on your keyboard. It is useful to know all the available ASCII values in order to be able to manipulate the characters in strings. For example, you could perform arithmetical operations using ASCII values in order to encrypt the characters in a password. There are 128 characters in the standard ASCII table numbered from 0 to 127 and there are 256 characters in the 'extended' ASCII table numbered from 0 to 255. There are also multibyte character sets which include higher values needed to represent characters in Japanese, Chinese and other languages with very large numbers of characters. But here I will stick to the basic ASCII character set.

In a `switch` statement you may optionally specify a `default` which will execute if no match is made by any of the `case` tests. In the *SwitchCase* project, I use a `for` loop to count through values from 0 to 127 and display the ASCII character which that number represents. At each turn through the loop, I use a `switch` statement to try to categorise the type of each character to show whether, for example, it is a Space character, a Tab character or a number. Here is my `findchartype()` function which contains a `switch` test to try to categorise characters with an ASCII value given by the `int` variable `i`:

SwitchCase

```
void findchartype(int i) {
    switch (i) {
    case 0:
        chartype = "Null";
        break;
    case 7:
        chartype = "Bell";
        break;
    case 8:
        chartype = "BackSpace";
        break;
    case 9:
        chartype = "Tab";
        break;
    case 10:
        chartype = "LineFeed";
        break;
    case 13:
        chartype = "Carriage Return";
        break;
    case 32:
        chartype = "Space";
        break;
    case 48:
    case 49:
    case 50:
    case 51:
    case 52:
    case 53:
    case 54:
    case 55:
    case 56:
    case 57:
        chartype = "Number";
        break;
    default:
        chartype = "Character"; // This is a single line comment
        break;
    }
}
```

Note that here `chartype` is a 'string' variable – or, to be more accurate, it is a pointer to a character (this is explained in Chapter 7) which has been declared like this:

```
char *chartype;
```

In the preceding example, if the `int` variable `i` is `0`, it matches the first `case` test and the string variable `chartype` will be assigned the value `"Null"`:

```
case 0:
    chartype = "Null";
    break;
```

Then the keyword `break` is encountered so no more tests are done. Similar tests and assignments are performed when `i` has the values 7, 8, 9, 10, 13 or 32. If `i` has any value between 48 and 57, the string "Number" is assigned to the `chartype` variable. That is because there is no `break` after any of the `case` values from 48 to 56, so if any match is made with one of those values the execution 'trickles down' through all the other `case` blocks until it meets the first `break` statement – this occurs after `case 57`:

```
    case 48:
    case 49:
    case 50:
    case 51:
    case 52:
    case 53:
    case 54:
    case 55:
    case 56:
    case 57:
        chartype = "Number";
        break;
```

If `i` has any other value – that is, any value that does not match one of the numeric case values, the code in the `default` section is run, and "Number" is assigned to `chartype`:

```
    default:
        chartype = "Character";
        break;
```

Strictly speaking you don't need to put a `break` in the `default` section. However, it is generally considered to be good practice to do so. In fact, in some cases, failing to do so will cause some weird problems. As we'll see next.

switch/break Bugs

In my examples, I have put the test values in my `switch` statements in what seemed like some sort of logical order: 48, 49, 50 and so on. In fact, the order is not significant and once your code has been compiled, it will not necessarily be evaluated in the order in which it was written. I could order my tests: 50, 48 and 49, and the end result would be the same. I could even put the `default` section somewhere in the middle of the tests instead of (as is more usual) right at the end.

Look at this code:

SwitchBug

```
#include<stdio.h>

void switchtest(int x) {
    int i = 0;

    switch (x) {
    case 0:
        i += 0;
        break;
    case 1:
        i += 1;
        break;
    default:
        i += 100;
    case 2:
        i += 2;
        break;
    }
    printf("x=%d, i=%d\n", x, i);
}

int main(int argc, char** argv) {
    for (int i = 0; i < 4; i++) {
        switchtest(i);
    }
    return 0;
}
```

My intention here is to test the value of `x` and add a number to the value of `i` (which I initially set to 0) just so long as the value of `x` is 0, 1 or 2. If it is any other value then my `default` section sets `i` to 100. When I test this, I find that I get exactly the results I expect for values 0 and 1:

```
x=0, i=0
x=1, i=1
```

But what about when `x` is 2? Since the `default` section is written above the `case` statement for the value 2, will `default` be executed and therefore stop `case 2` making a match? Well no, it doesn't. This is what I see:

```
x=2, i=2
```

This shows me that the sections of the `switch` statement are not order-dependent. If the test value is matched by a `case` statement then that `case` statement will execute no matter what its position happens to be within the `switch` block. And that's true for `default` also. Even though the `case 2` test occurs after the `default` section in my code, when the test value is 2, a match is made with `case 2` rather than with `default`.

However, that's not the end of the story. Remember I said that when no `break` occurs, the execution 'falls through' to subsequent `case` statements. Now that's the tricky thing. In my code when `x` is 3, no match is made by any `case` statement so the `default` section is executed. And this is what I see:

```
x=3, i=102
```

This is not the result I was expecting. The `default` section is supposed to set `i` to 100. In fact, a match was made with `default` and then the `case` statement following it (`case 2`) has also executed so `i` is first set to 100 and then 2 is added to that to give 102.

If you find this confusing, just bear in mind that this only becomes an issue if you forget to end a `case` or `default` statement with a `break`. I can fix the problem in my code by adding a `break` to the `default` section:

```
default:
    i += 100;
    break;
```

Now when I run the code, I get the expected result:

```
x=3, i=100
```

case: evaluation order

My test shows that, even though the individual `case` statements are not initially evaluated in the order in which they are written in my source code, as soon as a match has been made, any `case` statements following the match (up to the first `break`) *are* executed in order.

chars and ints

In C, the `char` data type is compatible with the `int` data type since each character is defined by an integer value. This means that, instead of using an `int` value in a `switch...case` statement to determine the value of a character based on its integer (ASCII) value, you could use a `char` argument. To show an example of this, I have written a function called `findchartype2()` that does this.

This function declares a `char` parameter, `c`. The expressions in the `switch...case` block attempt to match `c` with `char` rather than `int` values (that is, with characters such as '0' and '1' between single quotation marks, or non-printing characters preceded by \ such as the null character `'\0'`, the Tab character `'\t'` and the linefeed character `'\n'`):

SwitchCase

```
void findchartype2(char c) {
    switch(c) {
        case '\0':
            chartype = "Null";
            break;
        case '\t':
            chartype = "Tab";
            break;
        case '\n':
            chartype = "LineFeed";
            break;
        case '\r':
            chartype = "Carriage Return";
            break;
        case ' ':
            chartype = "Space";
            break;
        case '0':
        case '1':
        case '2':
        case '3':
        case '4':
        case '5':
        case '6':
        case '7':
        case '8':
        case '9':
            chartype = "Number";
            break;
        default:
            chartype = "Character";
            break;
    }
}
```

Ranges

Instead of writing separate `case` tests for sequential values such as '0' to '9' or 48 to 57, as in the code examples we've seen so far, *some* C compilers let you specify a range of values in a single `case` test.

A range is defined by a start value and an end value separated by three dots. A match will be made when the test value (such as `i` or `c` in my examples) matches any values between the start and the end values of a range. For example, in the ASCII table, uppercase letters start with the value 65 ('A') and end with 90 ('Z'); lowercase letters start with the value 97 ('a') and end with 122 ('z'). So a C compiler that supports ranges would allow me to write these `case` statements to test an `int` value:

```
case 65 ... 90:
    chartype = "Uppercase Letter";
    break;
case 97 ... 122:
    chartype = "Lowercase Letter";
    break;
```

Similarly, I could use these statements to test a `char` value:

```
case 'A' ... 'Z':
    chartype = "Uppercase Letter";
    break;
case 'a' ... 'z':
    chartype = "Lowercase Letter";
    break;
```

Ranges make it easy to write simple multi-value test `switch` statements but they are not compatible with all compilers. If compatibility is important, use multiple `case` tests:

```
case 'A':
case 'B':
    // some code
    break;
```

Ranges are non-standard!

Bear in mind that not all C compilers permit this syntax. Ranges are an extension to standard C syntax and they are *not* universally supported.

5 – Functions

Functions provide ways of dividing your code into named 'chunks'. Once you create a named function, you may call it by that name and, if it declares any 'parameters', you may also pass matching pieces of data to the function. In this chapter we learn all about writing and using functions in C.

I've used functions many times throughout this book. In fact the block of code named `main()` that begins every program is itself a function. I've also used functions such as `printf()` and `fgets()` which are supplied, as standard, with the C compiler. And I've written my own functions, with names that I've chosen, such as the `readln()` function in the last chapter. In this chapter I'll explain functions in more detail.

What are functions for?

C programs are typically made up of many separate functions. Each function fulfils some specific task. For example, one function might do some type of calculation while another one might sort data items alphabetically. By putting the code for these tasks into a named function I can avoid repetition. Instead of rewriting the code every time I need to do a calculation or sort some data, I just 'call' the appropriate function by its name.

Function Declarations

A function is declared by specifying the data type of any value that's returned by the function (such as `int` or `char`) or `void` if nothing is returned. Then comes the name of the function, which may be chosen by the programmer. Then comes a pair of parentheses.

The parentheses may contain one or more 'arguments' or 'parameters' separated by commas. The parameter names are chosen by the programmer and each parameter must be preceded by its data type.

When a function returns some value to the code that called it, that 'return value' is indicated by preceding it with the `return` keyword.

Here are some example functions. First, a function that takes no arguments and returns nothing:

Functions

```
void sayHello() {
    printf("Hello\n");
}
```

This is a function that takes a single string (an array of `char`) argument and returns nothing:

```
void greet(char aName[]) {
    printf("Hello %s\n", aName);
}
```

This is a function that takes two `int` arguments and returns an `int`:

```
int add(int num1, int num2) {
    num1 = num1 + num2;
    return num1;
}
```

This is a function that takes two `double` arguments and returns a `double`:

```
double divide(double num1, double num2) {
    return num1 / num2;
}
```

Procedures, subroutines and methods

In some programming languages, functions that return nothing (`void`) may be called 'subroutines' or 'procedures'. In Object Oriented languages such as C#, Java and C++, functions that are 'bound into' objects are called 'methods'. C is not object-oriented so the term 'method' is not used. In fact, C programmers generally refer to all functions – both those that return values and those that do not – simply as 'functions'.

Calling Functions

To execute the code in a function, your code must 'call' it by name. In C, to call a function with no arguments, you must enter the function name followed by an empty pair of parentheses and a semicolon like this:

```
sayHello();
```

To call a function with arguments, you must enter the function name followed by the correct number and data-type of values or variables (separated by commas), like this:

```
greet("Fred");
divide(100, 3);
```

If a function returns a value, that value may be assigned (in the calling code) to a variable of the matching data type. Here, the `add()` function returns an `int` value and this is assigned to the `int` variable called `total`:

```
total = add(n1, n2);
```

The `divide()` function returns a `double` (floating point) value and this is assigned to the `double` variable called `result`:

```
result = divide(100, 3);
```

Arguments are Passed 'by value'

Pay close attention to the code in this function:

```
int add(int num1, int num2) {
    num1 = num1 + num2;
    return num1;
}
```

Notice that I have assigned the value calculated by the addition of the arguments `num1 + num2` to one of the arguments of that addition, `num1`. My code, in `main()` calls this function like this:

```
n1 = 10;
n2 = 3;
total = add(n1, n2);
```

When the variables `n1` and `n2` are passed to the `add()` function, their values (10 and 3) are assigned to the named parameters, `num1` and `num2` which are declared in the function:

```
int add(int num1, int num2)
```

Then the values assigned to `num1` (10) and `num2` (3) are added together and the result of that addition is assigned to `num1`:

```
num1 = num1 + num2;
```

Now `num1` has the value 13. So what is the value of `n1`? Recall that `n1` is the variable that was passed as an argument to the `add()` function. The value of `n1` was assigned to the `num1` parameter in that function. Since `num1` ends up with the value 13, does that mean that `n1` also has the value 13? When you run the code you will see that it does not. In `main()` I display the values of `n1` and `n2`, as well as the value returned by the `add()` function:

```
printf("%d + %d = %d\n", n1, n2, total);
```

This is the output:

```
10 + 3 = 13
```

As you can see, both `n1` and `n2` retain their original values (10 and 3). These variables are unaffected by changes made to the matching parameters in the `add()` function. That is because the C language passes arguments 'by value'. In other words when `n1` and `n2` are passed to the function `add()` it is only their values that are sent – here these are the integer values, 10 and 3. These values are 'detached' from the original variables. Any changes made to the values of the parameters within the function have no effect on the values of the variables outside that function.

By reference or by value?

If you have programmed in other languages you may know that sometimes changes made to parameters inside a function do indeed change the values of the variables that were passed as arguments to that function. When that happens we say that the parameters were passed 'by reference' (since the parameters refer to – and have an effect upon – the original variables) rather than 'by value' (in which case the parameters are assigned the values passed from the original variables but do not refer directly to those variables). I'll have more to say about passing 'by reference' in later chapters of this book.

6 – Arrays and Loops

In many programming languages, it is sufficient to think of an array as a high-level structure that can be used to store indexed lists of elements. In C, you also need to understand how arrays are stored in your computer's memory. In this chapter we look at how arrays are related to addresses.

We've already used arrays of characters in several projects in this book. For example, in Chapter 4, I wrote a function called `readln()`that created an array, `s[]`, of characters that were entered at the keyboard. Each character was assigned to the `char` variable `ch` and appended to the array at the index `i` like this:

```
s[i] = ch;
```

The end result was that if the user entered the characters 'H', 'e', 'l', 'l', 'o' these would be added sequentially to the array, `s[]`. The first character would be at the 'array index' 0, the second at index 1 and so on. You can think of an array as being like a container with a fixed number of slots numbered from 0 upwards like this:

Contents:	'H'	'e'	'l'	'l'	'o'
Index:	0	1	2	3	4

Notice that, since the first element in an array is at index 0, the last element is at the index given by the length of the array minus 1. In the array shown above, there are five characters so the array length is 5. The first element 'H' is at index 0 and the last element 'o' is at index 4, that is the position given by the array length 5 minus 1.

Array Elements

Arrays aren't restricted to storing characters. In C, an array can store other types of data as long as each element in the array is of the same data type. This is how to declare an array named `intarray`, that can store 5 integers:

```
int intarray[5];
```

When you want to access an element at a specific index in the array you can put the index number between square brackets like this:

```
intarray[3];
```

This lets you either obtain the existing value of the element at that index or assign a new value to that element. This is how I would assign the integer value 31 to the 4th element (that is, the element at index 3) of my array:

```
intarray[3] = 31;
```

You can initialize the values of an array by indexing them one at a time like this:

```
intarray[0] = 1;
intarray[1] = 11;
intarray[2] = 21;
intarray[3] = 31;
intarray[4] = 41;
```

The following line of code accesses the value from index 3 of the array:

```
printf("The integer at intarray[3] is: %d\n", intarray[3]);
```

Assuming the array has been initialized as shown above, this code displays:

```
The integer at intarray[3] is: 31
```

You can also initialize multiple elements of an array at the time it is declared. To do that you must assign a comma-delimited list of items enclosed by curly brackets like this:

```
int intarray[5] = {1,2,3,4,5};
```

In fact, when you initialize an array in this way, you don't need to specify the number of items between square brackets – the C compiler automatically creates an array capable of holding the specified number of items. Here I declare and initialize an array that contains five integers:

Arrays

```
int intarray[] = {1,2,3,4,5};
```

And here are arrays that contain four doubles and six chars respectively (the sixth `char` being a null 'string terminator'):

```
double doublearray2[] = {2.1, 2.3, 2.4, 2.5};
char chararray[] = {'h', 'e', 'l', 'l', 'o', '\0' };
```

Character arrays are very common in C (because they are used to define strings such as "Hello world"), and there is an alternative shorthand way of assigning a string to an array of chars, like this:

```
char chararray2[] = "world";
```

When a string is assigned in this way, the null character `'\0'` is appended automatically so you don't need to add it explicitly as you do when you assign characters one at a time.

What is a string?

Many programming languages define a string data type. C does not. In C a string is an array of characters (characters that are 'strung' together), ending with a null (zero) character. We'll be looking at strings and string operations in Chapter 7.

for Loops

One convenient way of iterating through the elements of array is provided by a `for` loop. You may recall that I explained the syntax of `for` loops in Chapter 2. In the next example, I iterate through the five-element `intarray`, counting from 0 to 4 – that is while `i` is less than (<) 5 – placing the value `i + 1` multiplied by 100 into each successive 'slot' of the array:

Arrays

```
for (i = 0; i < 5; i++) {
    intarray[i] = (i + 1) * 100;
}
```

Since `i` starts with the value 0, adding 1 to `i` gives 1. So here I multiply 1 by 100 which means that the value placed at index 0 of the array is 100. The values placed at successive positions in the array are: 200, 300, 400, 500.

while Loops

As we've seen, `for` loops are useful when you have a known number of items to iterate through – from 0 to 4, say. But sometimes you may not know in advance how many items you need to process. For example, you might write some code to format the lines in a text file. But each file may contain a different number of lines so you cannot assume, in advance, that there will be a specific number of lines to process.

while...

You may recall that we have used `while` loops before. In Chapter 4, when I had the problem of 'flushing' the user input, I used a `while` loop to carrying on reading any characters that the user had entered *while* more characters remained to be read:

```
void flush_input(){
    int ch;
    while ((ch = getchar()) != '\n' && ch != EOF);
}
```

Here is an example in which I prompt the user to enter a response 'y' or 'n'. I want a certain piece of code to keep on running if the user enters 'n' but to stop running if the user enters 'y'. Here is a `while` loop that does this:

```
while(c != 'y') {
    printf("\nEnter y or n: ");
    c = getchar();
    getchar();
      // ... code here to run until 'y' is entered
}
```

The code inside the block delimited by the curly brackets continues to run while the char variable `c` is not equal to (`!=`) 'y'. The user is prompted to enter a character which is read from input and assigned to `c`. When 'y' is entered, the test `while(c != 'y')` fails so the code stops running. If any other character is entered the test succeeds and the code runs once again.

Incidentally, you might wonder why I have a second call to the `getchar()` function. This is because after entering 'y' or 'n' the user presses the enter key. In fact, the characters entered are only transferred to my program once the enter key has been pressed. But the enter key itself adds a linefeed character to the end of the text that was entered.

My second call to `getchar()` simply 'mops up' this unwanted linefeed character. If you need a more robust way of reading characters from the keyboard, refer back to the `readln()` function from Chapter 4.

But let's assume that I decide that the default value of `c` should be 'y' and I initialize the variable with that value. What happens in this code?

WhileLoops

```
char c;

c = 'y';
printf("\ngetchar() with while loop...\n");
while(c != 'y') {
    printf("\nEnter y or n: ");
    c = getchar();
    getchar();
}
printf("\nThat's all folks!\n");
```

What happens is that the test `(c != 'y')` fails immediately because `c` *is* equal to 'y'. So none of the code inside the block between `{` and `}` can ever be executed. When it runs it displays this:

```
getchar() with while loop...

That's all folks!
```

'while' blocks run 0 or more times

As you can see from my example, there may be occasions when the code in a `while` block will never run. In other words, you might say that the code in a `while` block will execute 0 or more times. Here it happens to execute 0 times.

If you want to make sure that the code inside the block is executed *at least once* you can use a different variation: a `do...while` loop.

do...while Loops

A `do...while` loop begins with the keyword `do` and ends with the keyword `while` followed by the test condition.

The test is made at the end of the block of code rather than at the start so the code must necessarily run at least once. Here is my code rewritten with a `do...while` loop:

WhileLoops

```
c = 'y';
printf("\ngetchar() with do...while loop...\n");
do {
    printf("\nEnter y or n: ");
    c = getchar();
    getchar();
}while(c != 'y');
printf("\nThat's all folks!\n");
```

This code displays this:

```
getchar() with do...while loop...

Enter y or n:
```

Then it waits for me to enter a character. If I enter 'y' the test fails, the code block exits and this is shown:

```
That's all folks!
```

But if I enter any other character, the test succeeds (because `c` is not 'y'), the code block runs again and I am once again prompted to enter a character. And indeed, the loop continues running until I enter 'y'.

'do...while' blocks run 1 or more times

As the test comes at the end of a `do...while` block, the code in the block must run at least once. In other words, the code in a `do...while` block will execute 1 or more times.

In summary, the test condition comes at the end of a `do...while` loop but at the beginning of a `while` loop. This means that a `do...while` loop always executes *at least once* whereas a `while` loop *may never execute at all* if its condition evaluates to false the first time it is tested.

break and continue

There may occasionally be times when you want to break out of a loop right away – even if the loop condition does not evaluate to false. You can do this using the `break` statement. Just as `break` was used to make an immediate exit from a `switch...case` block (see Chapter 5), so too it will cause an immediate exit from a block of code that is run inside a loop. Look at this code:

```
int i;
i = 0;

while(i < 10) {
    if (i == 5) {
        break;
    }
    printf("i = %d\n", i);
    i++;
}
```

The `while` loop has been set to run as long as `i` is less than 10. But inside that loop I test if `i` is 5 and, if so, I exit the loop with `break`. This means that in spite of the `while` condition expecting to run the loop ten times (for values of `i` between 0 and 9) in fact, when `i` is 5 the loop stops running. The code following `break` is not run so this is what is actually displayed:

```
i = 0
i = 1
i = 2
i = 3
i = 4
```

Be careful when breaking out of a loop in this way. In a more complex loop, containing many lines of code, the `break` condition may not be obvious and it would be easy to assume that the loop would be guaranteed to run while `i` is less than 10. As a general principle, it is best (clearer and less bug-prone) to avoid breaking out of loops unless you have a good reason for doing so.

Let me turn to a more useful example of a loop that uses a `break`:

BreakAndContinue

```
char chararray[] = "Hello world! Goodbye";

void forbreak() {
    int i;
    char str[50];
    char c;

    // for loop #1 - encrypt string
    for (i = 0; i < 50; i++) {
        c = chararray[i];
        if (c == ' ') {
            str[i] = c;
            continue;
        }
        if (c == '!') {
            str[i] = '\0';
            break;
        }
        str[i] = chararray[i] + 1;
    }
    printf("Encrypted string is '%s'\n", str);
  }
```

Here the `forbreak()` function 'encrypts' a string (that is, the array of characters, "Hello world! Goodbye", stored in `chararray)` by adding 1 to the numeric (ASCII) value of each character. It creates a new string, `str`, from those encrypted characters:

```
str[i] = chararray[i] + 1;
```

Suffice to say, this is about as simple (and insecure) as an encryption algorithm can get. Real-world encryption algorithms are much more complex than this one! Even so, it serves to illustrate the basics of how to process strings, as well as arrays of other data-types, using loops.

The code here can handle strings up to 50 characters in length. In principle these might be strings entered at the keyboard or read from a file. For simplicity, however, I have created the string shown below in order to illustrate how the program works:

```
char chararray[] = "Hello world! Goodbye";
```

As I want each string to have a maximum length of 50 characters, I set up a `for` loop to iterate over the characters from 0 to 49. However, the actual length of each string might be less than 50. So I have made it a requirement that each string must be terminated by the `'!'` character. When that character is found the standard C string-terminator `'\0'` is substituted and the rest of the string is ignored because at that point I break out of the `for` loop:

```
if (c == '!') {
    str[i] = '\0';
    break;
}
```

This means that if a string has only 10 characters ending with `'!'` the `for` loop will run only ten times (it will then exit on `break`) even though the loop is set up to run 50 times.

continue

There is one other character – the space `' '` - that I want to treat specially. When a space is encountered – for example, the space character between the words "Hello world" – I want to retain that space character rather than encrypt it. This is how my code does that:

```
if (c == ' ') {
    str[i] = c;
    continue;
}
```

The `continue` statement is a bit like a less dramatic version of `break`. Whereas `break` exits the loop and *stops* running the code in the loop, `continue` exits *from the current iteration* of the loop but then carries on running the code in the loop.

So, in my example, if I break on `'!'`, the code in the loop stops running. Given the string `"Hello world! Goodbye"` the code would process up to the `'!'` character and no further.

But the code will continue running after it processes the space `' '`. That means it exits the loop when `' '` is found after "Hello" but then it continues running the loop to process the rest of the characters, "world".

The result is that my code encrypts the string `"Hello world"`, by adding 1 to the ASCII value of each character, so that 'H' becomes 'I', 'e' becomes 'f' and so on. But it leaves the space character unchanged:

```
Encrypted string is 'Ifmmp xpsme'
```

Let's suppose we've already encrypted a string and now we want to decrypt it. Here is another example of `break` and `continue` which translates the encrypted string (by subtracting 1 from each character value) back to the unencrypted version.

This time, it iterates over the characters in the encrypted string, `str`, and it then copies the unencrypted characters back into `str`. Since the space characters in that string are not encrypted, the code ignores spaces by executing `continue` when one is found. But it `breaks` when the string terminator `'\0'` is found:

BreakAndContinue

```
// for loop #2 - decrypt string
for (i = 0; i < 50; i++) {
c = str[i];
if (c == ' ') {
        continue;
    }
    if (c == '\0') {
        break;
    }
    str[i] = str[i] - 1;
}
printf("Decrypted string is '%s'\n", str);
```

So this time 1 is subtracted from the value of each character: 'I' becomes 'H', 'f' becomes 'e' and so on, but again the space is left unchanged. So the first loop encrypted "Hello world" to create the string "Ifmmp xpsme". Now this second loop decrypts the string "Ifmmp xpsme" – and this is the result:

```
Decrypted string is 'Hello world'
```

Use break and continue with care!

As with `break`, you should use `continue` with caution. There are perfectly good reasons for jumping out of code blocks using `break` or `continue` but, if over-used, jumps like this can make your code hard to understand and, in complex programs, they may result in subtle bugs.

break From while Loop

You can also break out of a `while` loop. Here is an example:

BreakAndContinue

```
void whilebreak() {
    int i;
    char c;
    char str[50];

    i = 0;
    while (i >= 0) {
        c = chararray[i];
        printf("[%d]='%c' ", i, c);
        if (c == '!') {
            str[i] = '\0';
            break;
        }
        str[i] = c;
        i++;
    }
    printf("\nAfter while loop, str='%s'", str);
}
```

This time my code runs a `while` loop with no valid end condition, since `i` will always be greater than or equal to 0:

```
i = 0;
while(i >= 0)
```

It displays the character and the index of each item in `chararrary` and it builds a new string that ends when the `'!'` character is found.

```
[0]='H' [1]='e' [2]='l' [3]='l' [4]='o' [5]=' ' [6]='w' [7]='o' [8]='r' [9]='l'
[10]='d' [11]='!'
After while loop, str='Hello world'
```

A loop with no valid end condition will run forever unless you explicitly `break` out of it. In this loop, when `'!'` is found it breaks:

```
if (c == '!'){
    str[i] = '\0';
    break;
}
```

Multi-dimensional Arrays

Before leaving the subject of arrays and loops, I want to mention multi-dimensional arrays. These are, in effect, arrays of arrays. You are not restricted to storing arrays that extend in single rows from 0 to some upper limit. You can also have arrays that can be thought of as having both rows and columns like a spreadsheet: one dimension stores the rows, the other dimension stores the columns.

How many dimensions?

Multi-dimensional arrays can have more than two dimensions: arrays of arrays of arrays. However, to keep things reasonably easy to understand, I'll stick to arrays with two dimensions.

Conceptually a two-dimensional array forms a sort of 'grid' and you will find an example of this in the *MultiDimensionArrays* project. Just as with single-dimensional arrays, you can initialize the elements of a multi-dimensional array but putting all the elements between curly brackets and assigning them to the array identifier at the time of its declaration.

When assigning the elements of a multi-dimensional array, you need to place one set of curly brackets (the 'outer array') around a comma-delimited list of curly brackets arrays (the 'inner arrays') each of which contains a comma-delimited list of array elements.

MultiDimensionArrays

```
int grid [3][5] = {
    {1, 2, 3, 4, 5},
    {6, 7, 8, 9, 10},
    {11, 12, 13, 14, 15}
};
```

In the example shown above, I have declared an array named `grid` that contains 3 arrays, each of which contains 5 integers. You can think of this as a sort of matrix with 3 rows and 5 columns. If this were a spreadsheet, the intersection of each row and column would form a 'cell' and the contents of each cell would be an integer: 1, 2, 3, 4 and so on.

1	2	3	4	5
6	7	8	9	10
11	12	13	14	15

Remember that each 'row' and 'column' is indexed from 0, so the first row is row 0, the second column is column 1 and so on.

	0	*1*	*2*	*3*	*4*
0	1	2	3	4	5
1	6	7	8	9	10
2	11	12	13	14	15

To access a specific piece of data I need to give its 'cell location' using square-bracket notation with the 'row' index in one pair of brackets and the 'column' index in another pair of brackets. This is how I would print out the value stored at row 1 and column 2 (counting from the start index 0, this gives the item on the second row in the third column):

```
printf("%d", grid[1][2]);
```

	0	*1*	[2]	*3*	*4*
0	1	2	3	4	5
[1]	6	7	**8**	9	10
2	11	12	13	14	15

So that prints the integer 8.

If you want to iterate over these arrays, you will need to iterate first over the 'rows' (the 'nested arrays') – for example, you could do this using a `for` loop like this:

```
for (row = 0; row < 3; row++)
```

This `for` loop initializes the `row` variable to the index of one of the 'nested' arrays on each turn through the loop. Now, in order to iterate over the items stored in each nested array (which you can think of as the 'columns' of the grid), you would need to have another `for` loop inside the first `for` loop, like this:

```
for (column = 0; column < 5; column++) {
```

In my sample code, this is how I iterate over all the items stored in my `grid` two-dimensional array and display the 'row' number followed by the 'column' numbers and data (the `int`) stored at that location:

MultiDimensionalArrays

```
int row;
int column;

for (row = 0; row < 3; row++) {
    printf("--- row %d --- \n", row);
    for (column = 0; column < 5; column++) {
        printf("column[%d], value=%d\n", column, grid[row][column]);
    }
}
```

This is what is displayed when the program runs:

```
--- row 0 ---
column[0], value=1
column[1], value=2
column[2], value=3
column[3], value=4
column[4], value=5
--- row 1 ---
column[0], value=6
column[1], value=7
column[2], value=8
column[3], value=9
column[4], value=10
--- row 2 ---
column[0], value=11
column[1], value=12
column[2], value=13
column[3], value=14
column[4], value=15
```

Now you might wonder what you would need to do in order to break out of the inner `for` loop? You can do this, just as you would break out of a `switch...case` block, using the keyword `break`.

But would the `break` cause you to exit from just the *inner* loop or would it exit from the *outer* loop too? Try it out. Look at the next example. Here I have added code to the inner loop that breaks when the value of `column` is 2:

MultiDimensionalArrays

```
for (row = 0; row < 3; row++) {
    printf("--- row %d --- \n", row);
    for (column = 0; column < 5; column++) {
        printf("column[%d], value=%d\n", column, grid[row][column]);
        if (column == 2) {
            break;
        }
    }
}
```

This time, this is what I see when the program runs:

```
--- row 0 ---
column[0], value=1
column[1], value=2
column[2], value=3
--- row 1 ---
column[0], value=6
column[1], value=7
column[2], value=8
--- row 2 ---
column[0], value=11
column[1], value=12
column[2], value=13
```

From this you can see that the inner loop breaks when `row` is 0 and `column` is 2 but the outer loop continues running and it breaks again when `row` is 1 and `column` is 2 – and so on. This shows that `break` causes an exit from the innermost loop only.

Breaking bad?

`break` works well – it is clear – when there is a single loop to be exited. `break` does not work so well – it is unclear – when there are nested loops (loops inside other loops). The aim of the programmer should always be to write *correct* and *clear* code. It's not how fast you can write code that is important – it's how fast you can debug it. Because you need to be sure that your code works reliably in all circumstances. Clarity in code costs nothing. Debugging time most certainly does.

Once again, I should emphasize that breaking in this way is not always the most elegant way of terminating a loop. Whenever possible, try to terminate a loop only when the loop condition is met – for example when the test in a `while` loop or the expression in the second part of a `for` loop (e.g. `column < 5`) evaluates to false.

But sometimes breaking from loops is an efficient way of getting out of some code that you want to stop running *immediately*. Experienced programmers make use `break` for efficiency. Inexperienced programmers may use `break` as a shortcut way of bypassing the logic of the test controlling the loop. Make sure you understand the difference!

7 – Strings and Pointers

The most important thing to know about the string data-type in C is that there isn't one! Many other languages such as Java, C# and Pascal have a string type that lets you create variables to which string literals such as "Hello world" may be assigned. That isn't possible in C. As a consequence, C strings pose certain programming problems that you will not encounter in most other modern languages.

Even though we've used strings many times in this book, I have never created a variable of the `string` type because that type doesn't exist. Instead I have created strings like this:

StringIndex

```
char str1[] = "Hello";
```

Remember that a string is always terminated by a null `'\0'` character. It turns out that when you initialize a string at the time of its declaration, as in the example above, a null terminator is added automatically. The first null terminator found in a string will be treated as the end of that string. Look at this declaration:

```
char str2[] = "Goodbye\0 world";
```

What will I see when I display `str2` with `printf()`, like this?

```
printf("%s\n", str2);
```

This is what is displayed:

```
Goodbye
```

That is because the string terminates on the `'\0'` character which is embedded into the string `"Goodbye\0 world"`:

Arrays and Pointers

In C, I can declare and initialize strings either by placing a pair of square brackets after an identifier or by preceding the identifier with an asterisk * like this:

StringsAndPointers

```
char str1[] = "Hello";
char *str2 = "Goodbye";
```

At first sight, these two declarations appear to be more or less equivalent. Each is initialized with a string and I can display that string using `printf()` like this:

```
printf("%s\n",  str1);
printf("%s\n",  str2);
```

In fact, the apparent similarity is deceptive. In order to understand why that so, we now have to get to grips with one of the most challenging aspects of the C language – pointers.

In the example above, the asterisk (or 'star') indicates that the variable `str2` is a pointer to some memory location. In this case, this happens to be the memory location where the array of characters forming the string "Goodbye" is stored.

* The confusing 'star'

C programmers often refer to the asterisk character '*' as a 'star' when it is used with pointer variables. The asterisk is, of course, also used as the multiplication operator. Don't get them confused! A variable such as `str2` that is declared after a star (as in `char *str2`) is a pointer.

Addresses

Each piece of data in your computer's memory is stored at some memory location or 'address'. You can display that address using the 'address-of' operator `&` placed before a variable name. This is how I would display the addresses of `str1` and `str2`:

```
printf("%d\n", &str1);
printf("%d\n", &str2);
```

If you ran this code, it would display some numbers such as:

```
2686746
2686740
```

These are the addresses – the locations in computer memory – where the `str1` variable and the `str2` array live. Now that we have their addresses, let's take a look at their values – that is, the data that is stored at those addresses. Here I will print out the address of `str1` and `str2` followed by its value shown first as an integer (`%d`) and then as a string (`%s`):

```
char str1[] = "Hello";
char *str2 = "Goodbye";

printf("%d %d %s\n", &str1, str1, str1);
printf("%d %d %s\n", &str2, str2, str2);
```

Below you can see what is displayed – though the actual numbers will almost certainly be different if you run this code. That's because the addresses (or 'locations') in your computer's memory won't be the same as they are on my computer:

```
2686746 2686746 Hello
2686740 4206628 Goodbye
```

This tells me that the address of `str1` is 2686746 and its value expressed as an integer *is the same number*: 2686746. Its value when expressed as a string is the string with which it was initialized, "Hello".

The *address* of `str2` is 2686740 but its *value* expressed as an integer is *a different number*: 4206628. Its value when expressed as a string is the string with which it was initialized, "Goodbye".

Arrays and Addresses

The important thing to observe here is that the value of the array name, `str1` when expressed as an integer is the same as the address of that name. In fact, we can say that:

The value of an array name is the address of the start of an array.

Displaying pointer values: %d or %p?

In some examples in this chapter, I use the decimal `%d` format specifier when displaying pointer values. It is generally considered more 'correct' to use the `%p` format specifier with pointers. I have avoided `%p` here for the simple reason that it displays numbers in hexadecimal (base 16) rather than decimal (base 10) format.

Some experienced C programmers may be so familiar with hexadecimal that they can count in hex numbers as easily as in decimal numbers. But for most people, most of the time, decimal numbers are easier to understand.

For example, you may not immediately understand how to add the hexadecimal numbers 6E, C8 and 1F4. But in decimal format, these numbers are just 110, 200 and 500.

So, even though `%p` is the 'standard' format specifier for pointers, I often use `%d` in my examples because it is simply easier to see what is going on when working with decimal numbers. This is particularly important when we need to 'count' the number of bytes that separate one element from another element – for example, in an array.

Pointers

Unlike an array name, the value of the pointer variable, `str2`, is not its *own* address. It is a *different* address. In my example, the *value* of `str2` is the address at which the string "Goodbye" begins. So, in summary, this is what we can say about these two identifiers:

```
char str1[] = "Hello";
```

address of `str1` = `2686746;`
address of `"Hello"` = `2686746;`

```
char *str2 = "Goodbye";
```

address of `str2` = `2686740;`
address of `"Goodbye"` = `4206628;`

In other words, the array name, `str1` and the string "Hello" are one and the same thing and they represent the same address:

NAME	DATA					
Data:	'H'	'e'	'l'	'l'	'o'	'\0'
Address:	2686746					

Array names compile to addresses

If you find it hard to understand how an array name and an address can be the same, just think what happens when your source code is compiled by the C compiler. When the compiler (and its associated tool, the linker) encounters an array identifier, (for example, `str1`), it *replaces* that identifier with an instruction to the loader (the tool which will eventually run the program) to *replace* the identifier with the address of the array. That address is now fixed. It cannot be changed during the execution of the program. But `str2` is a *pointer variable* which, just like any other variable, has its *own* address. Its *value* however, is the address of an array. And that value *can* change if new addresses are assigned to the pointer variable.

Pointer variables (such as `*str2`) are different from array identifiers (such as `str1[]`). The name `str1` can be regarded as a symbolic *equivalent* of the address of an array. But the pointer `str2` is a variable whose *value* is the address of an array.

In the example below, the string "Goodbye" occupies one address (`4206628`). The pointer variable `str2` occupies a different address(`2686746`). The *value* of `str2` (its data) is a number. And that number is the *address* of the string "Goodbye". So you can think of the pointer variable `str2` as *pointing to* the address of the string "Goodbye".

Data:	'G'	'o'	'o'	'd'	'b'	'y'	'e'	'\0'
Address:	4206628							

NAME	str2
Data:	4206628
Address:	2686746

Since a `char` array name, such as str1 gives the address where a string begins, that means it must also give the address of the first character in that array. So where are the other characters in the `char` array located? To understand that we need to understand offsets.

Arrays or pointers?

Before moving on, you need to be absolutely sure that you understand the differences between an array name such as `str1` (declared as `char str1[]`) and a pointer variable such as `str2` (declared as `char *str2`).

```
char str1[]
```

In brief, an array name such as `str1[]` represents the *actual memory location* where an array of characters (such as "Hello") is stored.

```
char *str2
```

A pointer such as `*str2` is a variable whose *value* is a number that gives the memory location where a character, or an array of characters, is stored.

Array Offsets

A `char` array, in common with any other array, is a series of items stored next to one another (contiguously) in memory. Each character in the array is located at a distance – an 'offset' – of one character's worth of memory after the character that went before it.

Offsets

An offset within an array is an integer value indicating the distance between one array element and another or the distance from the start of the array to the start of some element in that array.

The characters 'H', 'e', 'l', 'l', 'o' are placed one after the other in an array. That array starts with 'H'. So we can think of the array as existing at a location in your computer's memory that starts at the position or 'address' of the start of the array – that is, the address of the 'H' character.

Let's imagine that address of 'H' in this char array is (for the sake of simplicity) 100. Let's also imagine that the address of each subsequent character in the array goes up by 1. So the string "Hello" (terminating with the null `'\0'` character) can be thought of as living at these memory addresses:

Data:	'H'	'e'	'l'	'l'	'o'	'\0'
Address:	100	101	102	103	104	105

Array addresses in real programs

The example I give here is hugely simplified. Real addresses may have high values in memory. The address of each array element will increase by whatever amount of memory is needed to hold each item in the array.

When I declare a `char` array, `str1`, like this –

```
char str1[] = "Hello";
```

– the name `str1` indicates the 'address' of the start of the array. In my simplified example, that would be the memory location 100. My code can then treat each subsequent character in that array as a part of a complete string that only ends when a null character is found.

But what happens if I declare a `char` pointer variable like this?

```
char *str2 = "Hello";
```

This time the variable, `str2`, does not directly indicate the address of the start of the array. Instead it stores a *reference* to that address – that is: the *value* of the pointer variable is a *number* that corresponds to the position in the computer's memory of the `char` array "Hello". That number is used to find the address. Which is another way of saying that the pointer variable 'points' to that address.

Strings and Addresses

You can assign a `char` pointer variable to the address of an array (given by the array name) using the address-of operator `&`. Let's assume that you have an array `str1` and an array-pointer `str2`:

StringsAndAddresses

```
char str1[] = "Hello";
char *str2 = "Goodbye";
```

You can make `str2` point to `str1` using the `&` operator like this:

```
str2 = &str1;
```

You can also make `str2` point to `str1` simply using the array name (without the `&` operator) like this:

```
str2 = str1;
```

The end result is the same. In both examples above, following the assignment, `str2` points to the address of the array `str1`. That is because the array name itself, `str1`, gives the address of the array.

An array name is not a variable

In some C programming books, array names are described as 'variables'. That isn't correct. The value of an array name – for example, the address of a `char` array such as `str1` – is calculated after you compile and load your program. Unlike a variable, an array name cannot be assigned a new value when your program is running (though new values can be assigned to its individual elements). If an array name really were a variable, it would be possible to assign new values to it. That's what variables are for. This means that an array name is constant. It is *not* a variable.

Using Strings with Functions

You can pass a string to a function using either the character-array (square brackets) or character-pointer syntax (*). This is valid:

ReturnStrings

```
void string_function(char astring[])
```

And so is this:

```
void string_function(char *astring)
```

To return a string, you should declare the return-type of the function as `char *`. Here is an example of returning a string with a maximum length of 100 characters, defined by `MAXSTRLEN` (note that it is the programmer's responsibility to ensure that this length is not exceeded):

```
#define MAXSTRLEN 100

char greeting[MAXSTRLEN];

char *string_function(char astring[]) {
    strcat(greeting, "hello ");
    strcat(greeting, astring);
    strcat(greeting, "\n");
    return greeting;
}
```

strcat() alternatives

`strcat()` is one of those 'traditional' C functions that is now considered to be unsafe because your code may accidentally assign more characters to a string than have been allocated to hold the string. Your C compiler may provide safer alternatives but these may not be compatible with all other C compilers. In spite of its disadvantages, `strcat()` is a widely supported function which is why I use it in my code example.

Here the string to be returned is created using the `strcat()` function which concatenates one string with another. In this case, the `greeting` array that is returned from the function has been declared outside of the function itself.

I declare the greeting array outside the function to ensure that it continues to exist after we exit from the function. In other words, the greeting array is within the 'global scope' of my program. Scope will be explained in the next chapter. I can call this function like this:

```
printf(string_function("Fred"));
```

The result is that the function's return value is "hello Fred\n" and that is what displayed by printf(). But what if I want to return a string without first declaring a global array such as greeting? That's a bit more complicated. In order to do this safely, I have to set aside some memory to hold the string. I do this using the malloc() function which allocates space for my string on a global memory area called the 'heap'.

The stack and the heap

Each variable needs to have enough memory 'allocated' to store the data assigned to it. This ensures that other data aren't written into that particular piece of memory. Local variables, declared inside a function, are allocated memory in an area known as the stack. When you exit from a function, the variables on the stack are cleaned up. To all intents and purposes, they cease to exist. The malloc() function allocates space in a different part of your computer's memory called the 'heap'. The data assigned to variables allocated on the heap continues to exist even after you've exited the function in which they were allocated.

I have to tell malloc() how much memory – that is, how many 'bytes' – I need to be allocated. It doesn't matter too much if I allocate more memory than I need but it could be catastrophic if I allocate less memory than I need. In this case, I have decided to allocate 100 bytes (MAXSTRLEN), which is enough for 100 normal characters:

ReturnStrings

```
char *string_function_dynamic(char *astring) {
    char *s;

    s = malloc(MAXSTRLEN);
    s[0] = 0;
    strcat(s, "hello ");
    strcat(s, astring);
    strcat(s, "\n");
    return s;
}
```

Note that I have had to initialize the array `s` with a null character (assigning the integer 0 has the same effect as assigning the null char `'\0'`) before attempting to concatenate another string such as "hello" onto it.

Freeing memory?

It is good practice to free memory when no longer required. In small programs (such as this one), failure to free memory is unlikely to cause any problems. In large programs it might. Freeing memory is discussed in Chapter 10.

String Functions

There are various useful string functions in the standard libraries provided with your C compiler. You should include `string.h` in order to use these string functions:

```
#include <string.h>
```

Just about all C compilers provide functions to do common operations such as concatenating and copying strings. Many C compilers also provide numerous additional string functions. You should be sure to read the documentation for your C compiler to check on the full range of functions available.

Here I am going to show just a few of the traditional functions for use with strings and characters. These functions should be available with all commonly-used C compilers.

Strings or Characters?

Be careful when you enter string and character 'literals' – that is, string and character data such as `"Hello world"`, `"x"` or `'x'`.

A C string literal is placed between a pair of double-quotes whereas a `char` is placed between a pair of single quotes. Some functions that expect to operate on a `char` will, in fact, allow you to enter a string. But remember that a string – even one such as `"x"` that contains a single character – is really a memory location at which an array of characters begins. This means that if you accidentally enter the string `"x"` when you had intended to enter the `char 'x'` your code may not produce the expected results.

Look at this code which uses the `isalpha()` function to test if a `char` is an alphabetic character:

CharFunctions

```
if (isalpha('x')){
    printf("'x' is a letter");
}else{
    printf("'x' is not a letter");
}
```

When run, this displays:

```
'x' is a letter
```

But what happens if I accidentally enter the string `"x"` instead of the char `'x'`:

```
if (isalpha("x"))
```

In fact, the results now are somewhat unpredictable and may vary according to which compiler and build-options you are using. The Microsoft C compiler gives me a warning. If I ignore that warning, the program displays:

```
'x' is a not letter
```

The GCC compiler also gives a warning but then displays:

```
'x' is a letter
```

At any rate, using a string (an array of characters) when a `char` is expected is asking for trouble. It is incorrect and may cause all kinds of unexpected problems so be careful that you don't do it.

Common String Functions

Commonly used string functions include:

`strlen()` To find the length of a string.

Example:

StringFunctions

```
strlen("Hello")
```

Output:

```
5
```

`strcat()` To concatenate two strings:

Example:

```
#define MAXSTRLEN 200
char msg1[MAXSTRLEN] = "Result1: ";
strcat(msg1, "Easter");
printf("\n\nstrcat: '%s'", msg1);
```

Output:

```
strcat: 'Result1: Easter'
```

`strncat()` To concatenate a specified number of characters:

Example:

```
#define MAXSTRLEN 200
char msg2[MAXSTRLEN] = "Result2: ";
strncat(msg2, "Easter", 4);
printf("\nstrncat: '%s'\n", msg2);
```

Output:

```
strncat: 'Result2: East'
```

`strncpy()` To copy one string to another string

Example:

```
char myotherstr[6];
myotherstr[0] = 0;
strncpy(myotherstr, "Easter", 4);
printf("\nCopied this string: '%s'", myotherstr);
```

Output:

```
Copied this string: 'East'
```

`strstr()` To search for a substring (returned as a pointer) in a string

Example:

```
void searchstring(char searchstr[]) {
    char *ptrtostr;
    int foundat;
    ptrtostr = strstr(mystring, searchstr);
    foundat = (int)((ptrtostr - mystring) + 1);
    if (ptrtostr != NULL)
        printf("\n'%s' found at position %d\n", searchstr, foundat);
    else
        printf("\n'%s' not found\n", searchstr);
}
```

Output: Assuming `mystring` is "On the 2nd day of Christmas my true love gave to me, 2 turtle doves and a partridge in a pear tree." and `searchstr` is "2nd":

```
'2nd' found at position 8
```

String functions and memory

When copying or concatenating strings, you need to ensure that the destination string has enough memory to hold all the characters after the operation (including the final null '\0' character). In my code, I declare the destination strings with a fixed length like this:

```
#define MAXSTRLEN 200
char msg1[MAXSTRLEN] = "Result1: ";
```

C11 string functions

Some modern C compilers (mainly Microsoft C/C++) which support the 'C11' optional standard of the language provide a number of safer alternatives to the traditional C functions. These function names end with `_s`. They typically take additional arguments that help verify that only a fixed number of characters are used when, for example, copying or concatenating strings. This can help to avoid problems such as buffer overruns (as discussed in Chapter 4). Here is an example of using `strncpy_s()` to copy the string "Easter" to the `char` array `mystr` (defined as `char mystr[6]`). The second argument defines the size of the destination string and the fourth argument defines the number of characters to copy – the end result is that `mystr` is assigned the characters: "East".

```
strncpy_s(mystr, 6, "Easter", 4);
```

Common Char Functions

There are also some functions intended for use with single characters. To use these you will need to include `ctype.h`. These are the most common `char` functions. Each takes a `char` argument and returns a non-zero value representing true or zero if false:

`isalnum()`	An alphabetic letter or a digit
`isalpha()`	An alphabetic letter
`isblank()`	A space or tab character
`iscntrl()`	A control character
`isdigit()`	A digit
`isgraph()`	Any printing character except a space
`islower()`	A lowercase letter
`isprint()`	Any printing character including a space
`ispunct()`	A printing character: not a space or alphanumeric
`isspace()`	A whitespace character (`' '`, `'\n'`, `'\t'`, `'\v'`, `'\r'`, `'\f'`)
`isupper()`	An uppercase letter
`isxdigit()`	A hexadecimal digit

You can use these functions to test characters. The `chartypes()` function counts the occurrences of upper and lowercase characters, digits, blanks and punctuation:

CharFunctions

```
char mystring[] = "On the 2nd day of Christmas my true love gave to me, 2 turtle
doves and a partridge in a pear tree.";

void chartypes() {
    int i;
    char c;
    int numDigits = 0;
    int numLetters = 0;
    int numUpCase = 0;
    int numLowCase = 0;
    int numSpaces = 0;
    int numPunct = 0;
    int numUnknown = 0;
    int lengthOfStr;

    lengthOfStr = strlen(mystring);
    for (i = 0; i < lengthOfStr; i++) {
        c = mystring[i];
        if (isalpha(c)) {
            numLetters++;
            if (isupper(c)) {
                printf("'%c' [uppercase character]\n", c);
                numUpCase++;
            } else {
                printf("'%c' [lowercase character]\n", c);
                numLowCase++;
            }
        } else if (isdigit(c)) {
            printf("'%c' [digit]\n", c);
            numDigits++;
        } else if (ispunct(c)) {
            printf("'%c' [punctuation]\n", c);
            numPunct++;
        } else if (isblank(c)) {
            printf("'%c' [blank]\n", c);
            numSpaces++;
        } else {
            printf("'%c' [unknown]\n", c);
            numUnknown++;
        }
    }

printf("This string contains %d characters: %d letters (%d uppercase, %d
lowercase)\n",lengthOfStr, numLetters, numUpCase, numLowCase);

printf("%d digits, %d punctuation characters, %d spaces and %d unclassified
characters.\n", numDigits, numPunct, numSpaces, numUnknown);
}
```

In this sample program, the `main()` function simply calls the `chartypes()` function:

```
int main(int argc, char **argv) {
    chartypes();
    return 0;
}
```

Here is just some of the output:

```
'O' [uppercase character]
'n' [lowercase character]
' ' [blank]
't' [lowercase character]
'h' [lowercase character]
'e' [lowercase character]
' ' [blank]
'2' [digit]
'n' [lowercase character]
'd' [lowercase character]
' ' [blank]
'd' [lowercase character]
```

8 – User Defined Types and Scope

Sometimes you may need to store 'records' that contain multiple data fields. In C you can do that using structs. You may also want to create groups of named constants. For that you will need enums. In this chapter we look at structs and enums, scope and header files.

You might want to create a program that stores a 'database' of some sort – maybe books, DVDs, MP3 files, your old vinyl records or your CD album collection. Here, I'll assume you are cataloguing your CDs. Each album would need to include the following data items: the CD name, the recording artist, the number of tracks and a user-rating.

structs

The problem is that, unlike `char` or an `int`, a `CD` is not a data type that C recognizes. This is not a major problem, though, because you can create user-defined data-types in the form of structures or `structs`. Here I've created a `struct` that is capable of holding all the data items for a CD:

Structs

```
struct cd {
    char name[50];
    char artist[50];
    int trackcount;
    int rating;
};
```

struct declarations

To declare a `struct`, begin with the keyword `struct` followed by a pair of curly brackets. Between the curly brackets, put a semicolon-delimited list of one or more variables. The closing curly bracket should be followed by a semicolon.

Once a named struct has been declared you can create variables of the type of that named struct. This is how you might declare a simple cd variable called thiscd and a ten-element cd array variable called cd_collection:

```
struct cd thiscd;
struct cd cd_collection[10];
```

struct variables

To declare a struct variable, begin with the keyword struct followed by the struct name (such as cd, which you defined earlier), then a variable name (such as thiscd) and a semicolon.

A struct definition (such as cd) acts as a blueprint from which multiple struct variables may be created. You can think of each struct as a data 'record' and each of its variables as 'fields' in that record.

To access the fields you must enter the struct variable name, then a dot, then the field name – for example, thiscd.name or thiscd.artist.

In the sample project, *Structs*, I create an array of cd structs called cd_collection, from 0 to an upper limit defined by the constant NUMBER_OF_CDS:

```
#define NUMBER_OF_CDS 4
struct cd cd_collection[NUMBER_OF_CDS];
```

Just as you can access the data fields using the field name after a dot, so too you can assign values to those fields using dot-notation like this:

```
thiscd.trackcount = 20;
thiscd.rating = 10;
```

If the structs are stored in an array, you can access each element of the array using an array index between square brackets – for example, cd_collection[0] accesses the first element of the cd_collection array, at index 0 – and you can then assign values like this:

```
cd_collection[0].trackcount = 20;
```

In the sample program *Structs*, this is how I assign data to the fields of four `cd` records stored in the `cd_collection` array:

Structs

```
strcpy(cd_collection[0].name, "Great Hits");
strcpy(cd_collection[0].artist, "Polly Darton");
cd_collection[0].trackcount = 20;
cd_collection[0].rating = 10;

strcpy(cd_collection[1].name, "Mega Songs");
strcpy(cd_collection[1].artist, "Lady Googoo");
cd_collection[1].trackcount = 18;
cd_collection[1].rating = 7;

strcpy(cd_collection[2].name, "The Best Ones");
strcpy(cd_collection[2].artist, "The Warthogs");
cd_collection[2].trackcount = 24;
cd_collection[2].rating = 4;

strcpy(cd_collection[3].name, "Songs From The Shows");
strcpy(cd_collection[3].artist, "The Singing Swingers");
cd_collection[3].trackcount = 22;
cd_collection[3].rating = 9;
```

I've written the function `display_cdcollection()` which uses a `for` loop to display the data from each field of each `struct` in the array:

```
void display_cdcollection() {
    int i;
    struct cd thiscd;

    for (i = 0; i < NUMBER_OF_CDS; i++) {
        thiscd = cd_collection[i];
        printf("CD #%d: '%s' by %s has %d tracks. My rating = %d\n",
                i, thiscd.name, thiscd.artist, thiscd.trackcount, thiscd.rating);
    }
}
```

When this function runs, this is what is displayed:

```
CD #0: 'Great Hits' by Polly Darton has 20 tracks. My rating = 10
CD #1: 'Mega Songs' by Lady Googoo has 18 tracks. My rating = 7
CD #2: 'The Best Ones' by The Warthogs has 24 tracks. My rating = 4
CD #3: 'Songs From The Shows' by The Singing Swingers has 22 tracks. My rating =
9
```

Pointers to structs

You will often see the fields of structs being accessed using the `->` operator instead of a dot. The `->` operator is used like this: `cdptr->name` or `cdptr->artist`. The `->` operator is used with pointer variables. This will be explained in Chapter 10.

typedef

In the last example, I created a new data-type defined by a `struct` which I called `cd`. But, unlike standard data types such as `char` and `int` I was not able to create new `cd` variables just by preceding the variable name with the type name. So this was not allowed:

```
cd thiscd;
```

Instead I had to precede the variable declaration with the keyword `struct`, like this:

```
struct cd thiscd;
```

In fact, there is a way of creating new types that allow the declaration of variables using the same syntax as you would use for standard types. To do this you must explicitly define a type using the keyword `typedef`.

By tradition it is normal to name defined types with an initial capital such as `Mytype` or `Yourtype`. This is how I declare a type named `CD` (in uppercase) which identifies my `struct` named `cd` (in lowercase):

Typedefs

```
typedef struct cd CD;

struct cd {
    char name[50];
    char artist[50];
    int trackcount;
    int rating;
};
```

Alternatively, you can combine the typedef with the struct declaration like this (where the typedef name is placed after the closing curly bracket):

```
typedef struct cd {
    Str50 name;
    Str50 artist;
    int trackcount;
    int rating;
} CD;
```

Having done this I can now create CD variables like this:

```
CD thiscd;
```

And I can declare an array of CD records like this:

```
CD cd_collection[NUMBER_OF_CDS];
```

You can also typedef standard types such as int or char. In principle, this may provide an 'alias' in the interests of readability. In my sample program I have provided an alias, Str50, for a 50-element char array:

```
typedef char Str50[50];
```

I have used this alias when declaring the string fields of my cd struct:

```
Str50 name;
Str50 artist;
```

enums

Sometimes your programs may need to work with a fixed set of related values – for example, a calendar program may need to deal with the seven days of the week, whereas a gambling program might deal with four suits of playing cards.

In order to represent these values you could use integers from 0 to 6 for days or from 0 to 3 for suits of cards respectively. But often it would be clearer to use named identifiers instead of numbers.

Consider this code:

```
if ((card == 0) || (card == 1)) {
    printf("This card is red.\n");
```

It is not at all obvious what the 0 and the 1 are supposed to represent. If you use named identifiers, the above code could be rewritten like this:

```
if ((card == Hearts) || (card == Diamonds)) {
    printf("This card is red.\n");
```

There is a simple way to create series of descriptive identifying names such as Hearts, Diamonds, Spades and Clubs. You do so by creating an 'enumerated type' or `enum`. This is how I would define the four suits of a deck of cards:

```
enum suits {
    Hearts, Diamonds, Clubs, Spades
};
```

Now, when I want a variable of the `suits` 'type' I can create it like this:

```
enum suits playingcard;
```

Similarly, I could define an `enum` of the days of the week:

```
enum days {
    Monday, Tuesday, Wednesday, Thursday, Friday, Saturday, Sunday
};
```

And I could create a variable of that type like this:

```
enum days today;
```

When I want to assign a value to that variable, I can use one of the identifiers listed in the `enum` definition like this:

```
today = Saturday;
```

By default, the identifiers in an `enum` are assigned integer values from 0 upwards. So in my `days enum`, `Monday` has the value 0, `Tuesday` has the value 1 and so on.

You may also assign specific values to each identifier in an `enum` at the time of declaration. Here, for example, I assign numerical values that correspond to the name of each constant:

```
enum numbers {
    Couple = 2, Dozen = 12, Score = 20
};
```

Enumeration constants

The identifiers listed in an `enum` are actually constants because their values cannot be changed. An `enum` may sometimes be described as an 'enumeration constant'.

If you want to pass `enum` values to functions, be sure to declare the function argument appropriately. For example, here I declare a function that expects an argument `num` of the `enum` type `numbers`:

```
void buyinbulk(enum numbers num) {
   printf("The customer wants to buy %d items.\n", num);
}
```

I have rewritten my CD Database program using an `enum` to represent the user rating of each `CD` record. This is my `enum`:

Enums

```
enum score {
    Terrible, Bad, Average, Good, Excellent
};
```

This is my `CD struct` definition (note the `enum score` variable):

```
typedef struct cd {
    Str50 name;
    Str50 artist;
    int trackcount;
    enum score rating;
} CD;
```

This is an example of the assignment of a `rating` to the first `CD` record, at index 0, in the `cd_collection` array:

```
cd_collection[0].rating = Excellent;
```

Header Files

Real-world C programs are typically composed of many separate source-code files. Even a simple "Hello world" program such as the very first program from Chapter 2 of this book, makes use of code from more than one file. That's because, even though I entered all of my code into a single file, I also imported code from another file:

```
#include <stdio.h>
```

The code shown above tells the compiler to 'include' (that is, to make available to my program) the contents of the file named `stdio.h`. This is one of the standard 'library' files supplied with C compilers. The angle brackets < > tell the compiler to search for this file in the locations reserved for the standard library files. When the file is found, its contents are inserted (just as though you had copied and pasted them) at the point in your source file where it is included.

A file with the extension '.h' is called a 'header file'. A header file typically contains definitions of functions and constants. The header file normally does not contain the implementation of functions – only their declarations. The implementations are generally contained in source code files that end with the extension '.c'.

#include < > or " " ?

To include header files supplied as standard with a C compiler, use angle brackets like this:

```
#include <string.h>
```

To include header files from the current directory – that is, files that you have created within the current project, use double-quotes like this:

```
#include "mystring.h"
```

While you should always include the header files that define the functions and constants you need, you may be surprised to discover that sometimes you will be able to use functions which are declared in header files even if you forget to include those header files. This is because the C compiler may have 'compiled in' the C source code files containing the implementation of the functions.

Also, the C linker (see below) will sometimes find the names of functions that you have not declared in various libraries that it searches. However, if you don't include the header file that defines those functions, the compiler will not be able to check that all the data-types used by the function-calls in your program – that is, the types of the data returned from functions or passed to functions as arguments – are correct.

Compiling and Linking

To understand why header files are important, you need to understand how your C source code files are translated into executable programs. This is done in three steps:

Step 1: The Preprocessor
First your files are pre-processed. The pre-processor is a tool that processes with all the special commands preceded by a hash `#` character – such as `#define` to define 'constants' and `#include` to include header files.

Step 2: The Compiler
Then all the C source-code files in your program are compiled. The compiler translates the source code into an intermediate code format called 'object code' and this object code is saved into a number of separately compiled files called 'object files'. For convenience, these object files can be accumulated into an 'object library'.

Step 3: The Linker
Finally, all the separately compiled files are combined in a process called 'linking'. This is when the final executable program is created. This executable program contains 'machine code' – that is, code which is capable of being run by your computer hardware. The linker additionally 'links in' code from any object libraries required, for example the code for the `printf()` function.

Bear in mind that at *Stage 2* - the compilation stage - the compiler processes each source code file separately. You might have one file that contains a function called `xxx()` and nine other files that *call* the `xxx()` function. Since the compiler processes each file one at a time, it cannot verify that the implementation of `xxx()` in one file matches the function-calls to `xxx()` in all the other files.

The file *containing* the `xxx()` function and the files *calling* the `xxx()` function are only put together in the final stage – by the linker. By that time, if there are any problems, it's too late to fix them.

But if you include a header file that defines exactly what types of arguments the `xxx()` function takes and what data-type, if any, it returns, then the compiler will be able to refer to the definition in the header file. When it compiles each code file it can verify that it uses the same definition of `xxx()`specified in the header file. If a file does not use the correct definition, the compiler can spot the problem and show a warning message.

In the *HeaderFiles* sample project, I have created a code file called *mystring.c*, which contains the `readln()` function from Chapter 4 and a version of the `searchstring()` function from Chapter 7. This is the code in the *mystrings.c* file:

(HeaderFiles) mystring.c

```
#include <stdio.h>
#include <string.h>
#include "mystring.h"

int readln(char s[], int maxlen) {
    char ch;
    int i;
    int chars_remain;

    i = 0;
    chars_remain = 1;
    while (chars_remain) {
        ch = getchar();
        if ((ch == '\n') || (ch == EOF)) {
            chars_remain = 0;
        } else if (i < maxlen - 1) {
            s[i] = ch;
            i++;
        }
    }
    s[i] = '\0';
    return i;
}

int searchstring(char searchstr[], char sourcestr[]) {
    char *ptrtostr;
    int foundat;
    foundat = -1;

    ptrtostr = strstr(sourcestr, searchstr);
    if (ptrtostr != NULL) {
        foundat = (int)((ptrtostr - sourcestr));
    }
    return foundat;
}
```

By placing these functions in their own file, it makes it easy for me to reuse them in different projects. The header file *mystring.h*, declares these functions plus a symbolic constant, `BUFSIZE`:

(HeaderFiles) mystring.h

```
#define BUFSIZE 100
int readln(char[], int);
int searchstring(char[], char[]);
```

Notice that it is not necessary to provide parameter names in the function declarations in a header file – only their types such as `char[]` and `int`. The *main.c* file includes this header file like this:

```
#include "mystring.h"
```

This file now has access not only to the functions declared in *mystring.h* but also to the `BUFSIZE` constant:

(HeaderFiles) main.c

```
#include <stdio.h>
#include "mystring.h"

char b[BUFSIZE];
char teststring[] = "Hello world";

int main(int argc, char **argv) {
    int i;
    int stringpos;

    printf("starting...\n");
    i = readln(b, sizeof(b));
    printf("b=%s; i=%d\n", b, i);
    stringpos = searchstring(b, teststring);
    if (stringpos > -1) {
        printf("'%s' found in '%s' at index #%d\n", b, teststring, stringpos);
    } else {
        printf("'%s' not found in '%s'\n", b, teststring);
    }
    return 0;
}
```

Header files enable type-checking

Put simply, when you define functions in a header file, that file can be used by the compiler as a reference document. As each individual source code file is compiled, the compiler refers to the definitions in the header file to make sure that all the source code files agree on the types of data sent to and returned from the functions they use. The declarations of functions in a header file help the compiler to find potential problems before they become bugs.

Scope

'Scope' describes the 'visibility' of the variables, functions and constants in your code. Every program is made up of elements with well-defined boundaries. These program elements may be anything from an entire code file to a single function – and each of these elements defines a 'scope'.

Local Variables

Variables that are defined inside a function are said to have 'local' scope. They only 'exist' within the function itself. Code outside the function cannot access local variables. In the example shown below, the variable `num` is local to `func1()` and so it cannot be used in `func2()`:

```
void func1(){
    int num;
    num = 100;
}

void func2(){
    num = 200;      // This is an error!
}
```

Parameter scope

The parameters declared between parentheses in a function header also have local scope within that function.

Global Variables

Variables that are defined outside a function (that is, in the main 'body' of the code file) are said to have 'global' scope. They are available to all the functions in the code file. In the example below, the variable `num` is global so both `func1()` and `func2()` can use it:

```
int num;

void func1(){
    num = 100;
}

void func2(){
    num = 200;
}
```

When a local variable is declared with the same name as a global variable, the local variable will be used instead of the global variable.

```
int num = 50;

void func1(){
    num = 100;
    printf(" %d\n", num);     // local variable value: 100
}

int main(int argc, char **argv) {
    func1();
    printf(" %d\n", num);     // global variable value: 50
}
```

Naming header files

While the name of a header file (such as *mylib.h* with the extension .h) often matches the name of a C source-code file (such as *mylib.c* with the extension .c) this one-to-one matching between header and source-code file is not obligatory.

For example, in the sample project *Scope*, I have one header file, *mystring.h*, which declares functions found in two source-code files, *mystring.c* and *mystringutils.c*.

Scope and External Files

The functions declared in source code files throughout a project are, by default, accessible to all the files in that project. In other words, they have global scope. As mentioned before, if you intend functions to be shared among multiple source files, it is good practice to declare those functions in a header file.

However, the header file declarations do not change the scope of the code in the other files. Even if they are not declared in the header file, functions in C code files have global scope by default and they will be available throughout your project. That's because the linker will find all those functions if it can and it will link them in to the executable program.

Static Functions

Sometimes you may want to make sure that the functions inside one file cannot be used by the functions in some other file. You can do that by declaring the functions using the `static` keyword. This ensures that the functions remain private – that is, that they are only accessible within the file in which they occur.

In the *Scope* project the `searchstring()` function in the file *mystringutils.c* is declared to be `static`:

Scope

```
static int searchstring(char searchstr[], char sourcestr[]) {
```

I have made this function static because I want it to be available only to the function named `findsubstring()` within the same code file. It is my intention that when someone wants to search for one string inside another they must call `findsubstring()`. The `searchstring()` function is only ever intended to be used by the `findsubstring()` function and I want to be absolutely sure that nobody can call `searchstring()` from some other code file. By making the function `static` I have, in effect, hidden it from external code files.

Local static Variables

When declared *outside* a function, static variables have the same scope as static functions. That is, they are only visible within the current source code file. Confusingly, however, the keyword `static` has a different meaning when it is applied to variables declared *inside* a function. A `static` variable inside a function retains its value between function calls.

Let's suppose you have a `static int` variable called `x` that is declared in a function called `addnumbers()` and `x` is initially assigned the value 0. Inside the function, some code increments the value of `x` by 1 each time the function is called. If the function is called three times, `x` will now have the value 3:

Scope (main.c)

```
void addnumbers(){
    static int x = 0;
    int y = 0;

    x++;
    y++;
    printf("In addnumbers() x=%d, y=%d\n", x, y);
}

int main(int argc, char **argv) {
    addnumbers();
    addnumbers();
    addnumbers();
    return 0;
}
```

This is the output that will be displayed when the program above is run:

```
In addnumbers() x=1, y=1
In addnumbers() x=2, y=1
In addnumbers() x=3, y=1
```

Relatively few programs are likely to need to make use of local `static` variables. But while `static` variables are somewhat esoteric, `static` functions are not. It is highly likely that programs of any complexity will want to make some functions private (that is, `static`) to ensure that they cannot accidentally be used by code in other files.

Block Scope

When variables are declared inside a block (that is, inside some code enclosed by a pair of curly brackets), those variables are local to the block. They cannot be accessed outside the block. The *BlockScope* project illustrates this.

Here the variable `i` is local to the block so the final `printf()` is invalid because `i` is out of scope at that point:

BlockScope

```
{
    int i = 0;
    printf("%d\n", i);
}
printf("%d\n", i); // <----- error
```

for Loop Variables

The iterator variable in a `for` loop is a special variety of block-scoped variable. If you declare the iterator variable within the block header, then that variable is scoped within the `for` loop and cannot be accessed outside the loop. Once again, the final `printf()` here is invalid because `i` is out of scope at that point:

```
for (int i = 0; i < 10; i++) {
    printf("%d\n", i);
}
printf("%d\n", i); // <----- error
```

Bear in mind, however, that the 'traditional' way of declaring `for` loop variables is to do so *prior* to the start of the loop. In that case, the variable *is* accessible outside the loop:

```
int i;

for (i = 0; i < 10; i++) {
    printf("%d\n", i);
}
printf("%d\n", i); // This is OK
```

The ability to declare and initialize a `for` loop iterator in the loop header itself was introduced in the C99 standard of the C language. While it is safer to restrict the scope of the iterator within the loop itself (as a general principle, the narrower the scope of a variable, the more immune it is from accidental side-effects), many C programmers continue to declare the variable in the traditional manner, outside the loop.

9 – Files

The CD database in the last chapter suffers from an enormous limitation: the CD records are 'hard-coded' into the application itself. There is no way to save new records to disk and reload them into memory later on. In this chapter we'll find out how to save and restore data to and from disk.

In order to be able to save data on disk I need to create files capable of storing that data. My CD database would need to store fairly complex data-types – structs containing multiple data fields. I'll get around to that in Chapter 10. Before we do that, however, we need to get to grips with the basics of using files in C: how to open and close files. And how to write simple text into a file and read it back into memory later on. That's what we'll be doing in this chapter.

Opening and Closing Files

A file on disk is a storage area containing data which may either be represented as a sequence of printable characters – a 'text file' – or else may be some other kind of digital representation of formatted data – a 'binary file'.

Before you can use a file in your program, you must 'open' it. A file may be opened for reading when you want to load data into memory. It must be opened for writing when you want to save data from memory into the file. It must be opened for reading *and* writing when you want to be able both to load and save data. When you have finished using the file you should 'close' it.

To open a file you can use the `fopen()` function. This takes the file name as its first argument, and some characters specifying the file access mode as the second argument:

```
FILE *fopen(
   const char *filename,
   const char *mode
);
```

File Access Modes

The file access mode lets you open a file for reading (`"r"`), writing (`"w"`) or appending to a text file (`"a"`). You can open a file for reading and writing (`"r+"`) for a file that already exists, or destructive reading and writing (`"w+"`) which means that the file is truncated to zero length – effectively its contents are deleted, when it is opened. When handling binary files you need to add the character '`b`' to these modes (`"rb"`, `"wb"` and so on). For the full range of supported file access modes, refer to your compiler's documentation.

File Access Mode Summary

`"r"` Opens for reading. If the file does not exist or cannot be found, the call to `fopen()` fails and 0 (or the predefined constant `NULL`) is returned.
`"w"` Opens an empty file for writing. If the given file exists, its contents are destroyed.
`"a"` Opens for writing at the end of the file (by appending). Creates the file if it does not exist.
`"r+"` Opens for both reading and writing. The file must exist.
`"w+"` Opens an empty file for both reading and writing. If the file exists, its contents are destroyed.
`"a+"` Opens for reading and appending. Creates the file if it does not exist.

When you open a file using `fopen()`, the function returns a pointer to a `FILE` structure which is often referred to as a 'file pointer'. You may then use that pointer with various functions to open and close the file or read and write data to and from it. If the file cannot be opened, 0 (or the predefined constant `NULL`) is returned.

Alternative file functions

Your compiler may support other file-handling functions such as `fopen_s()` which is more secure than `fopen()`. Not all compilers support all of these alternative file functions.

File Pointers

A file pointer is not, as you might imagine, a pointer directly into a file on disk. In C, `FILE` is a predefined structure that contains information about a file, such as the file mode and the current position in a file (when characters are being written or read to and from it) and when the end of the file is reached. A file pointer points to a `FILE` structure.

Text Files

You will find some examples of basic file operations in the *FileBasics* sample program, which opens and closes a text file, "*test.txt*", then reads and writes lines of text to and from the file. This program also shows ways of deleting the file contents and removing the file itself.

First I define constants to specify the maximum length of a line of text and the name of the file to be used in my code:

FileBasics

```
#define MAXSTRLEN 200
#define FILENAME "test.txt"
```

The `writelines()` function opens the file for writing. If the file does not exist, it is created. If it does exist, its contents are deleted before any data is written. Two lines of text are then saved into the file and the file is then closed:

```
void writelines() {
    FILE *fp;
    fp = fopen(FILENAME, "w");
    fputs("Hello world\n", fp);
    fputs("Goodbye Mars\n", fp);
    fclose(fp);
}
```

If the specified file can be opened, the `readlines()` function reads lines of text from the file while there are still more lines to be read and displays those lines on screen (`stdout`), closing the file when all lines have been processed. If the file cannot be opened (in which case the file pointer `fp` is `NULL`), an error message is displayed:

```
void readlines() {
    FILE *fp = fopen (FILENAME, "r");
    char line [MAXSTRLEN];
    if (fp != NULL) {
        while (fgets (line, sizeof(line), fp) != NULL) {
            fputs (line, stdout);
        }
        fclose(fp);
    } else {
        printf("File %s cannot be opened!", FILENAME);
    }
}
```

My `clearfile()` function opens a file for writing but does not write any data into it. Opening a file for writing has the effect of deleting the file contents, so this function erases the contents of the file but leaves the file itself present on disk:

```
void clearfile() {
    FILE *fp;
    fp = fopen(FILENAME, "w");
    fclose(fp);
}
```

My `deletefile()` function removes the file itself rather than just deleting its contents, by calling the `remove()` function. This returns 0 if successful (or -1 if it fails).

```
void deletefile() {
    if (remove(FILENAME) == 0) {
        printf("%s file deleted.\n", FILENAME);
    } else {
        printf("Unable to delete the file: %s.\n", FILENAME);
    }
}
```

Since I am reading one line at a time from a text file, it would be very simple to write a program that counts the number of lines that the file contains.

This is how I've done that:

FileStats

```
void linecount(char *fn) {
    int numlines = 0;
    char line[MAXSTRLEN];
    FILE *fp = fopen (fn, "r");
    if (fp != NULL) {
        while (fgets (line, sizeof(line), fp) != NULL) {
            numlines++;
        }
        fclose (fp);
        printf("%s contains %d lines of text.\n", fn, numlines);
    } else {
        printf("File %s cannot be opened!\n", fn);
    }
}
```

If I pass to this function the name of a text file containing some text, it displays the number of lines. If I pass the name of an empty file it tells me that the file contains 0 lines. And if I pass the name of a file that does not exist, it tells me that the file cannot be opened.

As this program reads one line of text at a time, I can treat those lines of text in the same way that I might treat lines that were entered by the user at the keyboard. For example, you may recall that in a previous program I wrote a function to search for substrings in a string entered by the user. I can use that same function to search for substrings in each line read from a disk file.

FileSearchStr

```
#include <stdio.h>
#include <string.h>

#define FILENAME "sonnet.txt"
#define MAXSTRLEN 200

static int searchstring(char searchstr[], char sourcestr[]) {
    char *ptrtostr;
    int foundat;
    foundat = -1;
    ptrtostr = strstr(sourcestr, searchstr);
    if (ptrtostr != 0) {
        foundat = (int)((ptrtostr - sourcestr));
    }
    return foundat;
}

void findstrings(char *fileName, char *ss) {
    FILE *f;
    int count;
    char line[MAXSTRLEN];

    f = fopen(fileName, "r");         // open file read only
    if (f == NULL) {
        printf("Can't open the file: '%s'\n", FILENAME);
    } else {
        count = 0;                    // initialize the count
        while (fgets (line, MAXSTRLEN, f) != NULL) {
            if (searchstring(ss, line) >= 0) {
                count++;
            }
        }
        printf ("'%s' was found in %d lines\n", ss, count);
        fclose(f);                    // close it
    }
}
```

FileSearchStr (continued)

```
int main(int argc, char **argv) {
    findstrings(FILENAME, "then");
    findstrings(FILENAME, "my");
    findstrings(FILENAME, "snodgrass");
    return 0;
}
```

These sorts of operations are is all very well if the files you are processing contain nothing but plain text. But how do you read and write more complex data such as the multi-field CD records in my CD database? That is the subject of the next chapter.

stdin, stdout, stderr

In most C programs, there are three predefined files which are opened by the operating system: `stdin`, `stdout` and `stderr`. These are `FILE` pointers that define the standard streams for input, output, and error output. By default, standard input is read from the keyboard, while standard output and standard error are printed to the screen.

It would be a good programming exercise to try writing your own functions to do certain operations on files and their contents. For example, you could write a function to read the text from a file one character at a time instead of one line at a time. You could use this function to count the characters or to change uppercase characters to lowercase. Or you could encrypt the text in the file just as we encrypted strings back in Chapter 6.

On the next page there is the listing of the *FileSearchStr* sample program which calculates the number of lines that contain a specified substring in a file.

10 – Binary Files and Memory

In this final chapter I want to consider a few of the special features – and problems – associated with binary files. That is, files that may contain non-text data.

A 'binary file' is a file that contains data which cannot be treated as plain 'readable' text. Often this may be a file that stores some sort of specially formatted data such as, for example, the data of the records (that is, the structs) in my CD database.

Sometimes files of this sort are called 'random access' files because they allow you to access records at selected locations (these locations are not really 'random' in spite of the name!) rather than reading data sequentially from the start to the end of the file.

Binary Files

Of course, all files – even text files – are binary because all files contain data made up of binary digits or 'bits'. But text files are so widely used that it is often convenient to treat them specially – in particular by assuming that the file contains readable characters arranged on lines that end with linefeeds.

In fact, if you wish, you can even treat a text file as a binary file. For instance, in the *ReadFile* project I open a text file in binary reading mode:

ReadFile

```
f = fopen(fileName, "rb");
```

Now, instead of processing its contents one line at a time, I read the entire file into memory and process it one character at a time. Essentially, I fill an array (a 'buffer') named `b` with the contents of the file, then I iterate over the characters and increment the variable `linecount` each time the newline `'\n'` character is found.

But that isn't the interesting part of this program. The really interesting part is the code that calculates the size of the buffer needed to hold the contents of the file. I don't know in advance how big the file will be so I can't declare a fixed-size array in my code.

Let's look at how this is done in detail. When I open a file with `fopen()` the function returns a `FILE` pointer (which, you may recall from Chapter 8, is a pointer to a `FILE` struct).

This pointer is assigned to the variable `f`:

```
FILE *f;
f = fopen(filename, "rb");
```

I can now use various functions with `f` to 'move' the file pointer to indicate the file position at which I want to read or write. This is called 'seeking' and my code does this by using the `fseek()` function to seek to the end of the file. To do this seek operation, I put the `SEEK_END` constant as the third argument:

```
fseek(f , 0 , SEEK_END);
```

You should note that even though this sort of operation is frequently described as 'moving the file pointer', the file pointer itself is not really being moved. The note below explains this.

Moving file pointers?

'Seek' operations are commonly described (for historical reasons) as 'moving a file pointer'. This doesn't mean that a `FILE` pointer variable (such as `f` in the preceding example) has been moved. The pointer variable f is unaffected when you perform a 'seek' operation; it continues to point to the same `FILE struct`. This `FILE struct`, contains a value that indicates a position within an actual disk file.

Confusingly, this value is often called a 'pointer' – sometimes it is called a pointer to a 'buffer' or to a 'stream', meaning the data contained within the file. It is not really a pointer at all, in the way we normally think of pointers in programming. In fact, this so-called 'pointer' is likely to be a simple number. When a seek operation is performed, that number is updated to refer to a new position in the file on disk. This 'pointer' is just a 32-bit (or 64-bit for large files) offset from the start of the file.

Now I can use the `ftell()` function to find the position of the file pointer. This position is given in bytes – with one byte per character – so the position here tells me how many characters are in the file and I assign that value to the `size` variable:

```
size = ftell(f);
```

To move the pointer back to the start of the file, I use the `rewind()` function:

```
rewind(f);
```

Memory Allocation

Finally I am ready to create a buffer – an array – capable of holding the number of characters in the file. To do this I need to create an array with enough space to hold the characters. I do this using the `malloc()` function to allocate `size` amount of memory and assign this to `b`, like this:

```
b = malloc(size);
```

Check the return from malloc()

If sufficient memory is available `malloc()` will return a pointer to that memory. Normally, with modern computers and with relatively simple programs it is difficult to run out of memory. However, it is always good practice to check that `malloc()` has done the right thing, as we do here (though you may need a more descriptive error message!):

```
b = malloc(size);
if (b == NULL) {
   printf("help!!\n");
}
```

For the sake of brevity we don't always do much error-checking in the sample programs with this book. But in real-world programs, you should!

I can fill this array with characters by reading the contents of the file using `fread()`:

```
items_read = fread(b, 1, size, f);
```

The arguments to `fread()` are:

1) `b` – the buffer or array into which the data will be read.
2) the size of each item to read – here `1` for a single `char`.
3) `size` – which is the number of items (here the number of characters) to be read.
4) `f` - the pointer to the `FILE struct` associated with the source data file. The returned value, `items_read`, gives the number of items that were read.

Integer types

You may notice that the `items_read` variable is declared as being of the `size_t` type:

```
size_t items_read;
```

It turns out that `size_t` is a defined type – that is, the C library uses a `typedef` to define `size_t` to be an `unsigned int`.

The C language recognises various integer types, some of which are 'signed' (they may have both plus and minus values), some of which are unsigned so cannot have negative values – and some of which have different upper and lower values.

For example, a `long` may be capable of holding a bigger range of values than an `int`, though these value ranges vary according to the compiler. In most cases, a simple `int` will suffice. However, as the C library defines the return value of `fread()` to be of the type `size_t`, that is what I have used here.

Once I've read in the data I need to close the file:

```
fclose(f);
```

Now I am ready to process the data in memory. I do this using a `for` loop to iterate through all the characters in the array `b` (from `i = 0`, while `i` is less than `size`), incrementing `linecount` whenever a newline character is found:

```
for (i = 0; i < size; i++) {
    if (b[i] == '\n') {
        linecount++;
    }
}
```

Freeing Memory

Right at the end of the *ReadFile* program I call `free()` on the buffer `b`. The `free()` function frees up the memory that was allocated with `malloc()`:

```
free(b);
```

If I didn't free up that memory, it would remain allocated – that is it would remain unavailable for use by anything else in my program. So even though I have finished using my buffer variable, `b`, once I exit the `readin()` function, the memory that I allocated would still be in use, taking up space that I might need for other things later on, unless I call `free()` to reclaim that memory.

Memory Leaks

Let's assume that I had forgotten to free the memory used by b in the `readin()` function. Since my local variable `b` is no longer available to me once I've left the function, I no longer have any way of getting at that chunk of memory. That's because I no longer have a variable that points to that memory location.

This is called a memory leak. In a short and simple program like this, a single memory leak may not cause any problems. But in a large program, if you accumulate numerous memory leaks your program may eventually run out of memory causing it to slow down or even to crash. So, when you allocate memory that you no longer need be sure to free it!

Garbage collection

Some programming languages such as Java, C#, Python and Ruby automatically free up unused memory in a process known as 'garbage collection'. A programming language that does garbage collection relieves the programmer from the responsibility of freeing memory explicitly but it also introduces some performance penalties (garbage collection may slow down your programs). The C language is often faster and more efficient than garbage-collected languages – but you must be careful to manage memory yourself and free up memory that is no longer needed.

Saving Records to Disk

In the final program in this book, *CDdatabase*, show how to save, load and modify a database of 'records' stored on disk.

This is a bigger program than those which I've created previously. It makes use of many of the techniques and functions from earlier chapters so, in addition to showing examples of file-handling, this program should also help you revise many of the topics described earlier on.

Before looking at the code, let me explain what this program, does. It maintains a database of CD records saved into a binary file called "*cd_database.bin*". It prompts the user to enter single-letter commands to view or modify the data in this file. The commands available are:

`a`	add a new record
`d`	display all existing records
`m`	modify a specific record
`n`	show the total number of records
`s`	save data from memory to a file on disk
`q`	quit

The program comprises three source code files: *main.c* which runs a loop to process the one-letter commands until 'q' is entered; *mystring.c* which contains my line-reading function `readln()`; and *cddb.c* which contains the bulk of the code to manipulate the CD database.

There are also two header files: *mystring.h*, which declares the functions in *mystring.c*; and *cddb.h*, which declares the functions in *cddb.c* as well as a string type `Str50`, the `CD struct` type and a globally available array `cd_collection`.

This is the *ccdb.h* header file:

(CDdatabase) cddb.h

```
enum score {
    Terrible = 1, Bad = 2, Average = 3, Good = 4,
    Excellent = 5
};

typedef char Str50[50];

typedef struct cd {
    Str50 name;
    Str50 artist;
    int trackcount;
    int rating;
} CD;

CD *cd_collection;
CD tempcd;

void create_cdcollection();
void display_cdcollection();
int number_of_records_in_db(char*);
void save_cdcollection(char*);
int cdarraylen;
void add_cd(char*);
void modify_cd(char*);
```

Actually `cd_collection` is a pointer to a `CD struct` which, in this program will be the address of an *array* of `CD` structs. In this sense, it is similar to a pointer to `char` which may define the start of an array of characters.

I use a `CD struct` called `tempcd` as a temporary storage area when I read in the data for a new `CD` as it is entered at the keyboard. An `enum` called `score` defines constants for the `CD` 'rating'.

Take time to read through the code of this project, as supplied in the source code archive. By now you have all the skills you need to understand this code. To see exactly how it works, I suggest that you run the code using a debugger. If there is anything you don't understand, this project gives you the chance to identify any programming topics that you may need to revise by rereading the appropriate chapters of this book.

Here I want to concentrate on a few functions and programming techniques which I have not used before. Let's look first at the `load_cdcollection()` function in the *cddb.c* code file. This is the function that loads data from the disk file. This function is called by the `display_cdcollection()` function when the user enters 'd' at the command prompt.

This is the code of the `load_cdcollection()` function:

(CDdatabase) cddb.c

```
static int load_cdcollection(char *filename) {
    FILE *f;
    int numrecs;
    int numrecsread = 0;

    numrecs = number_of_records_in_db(filename);
    f = fopen(filename, "rb");
    if (f == NULL) {
        printf("Cannot read file: %s\n", filename);
    } else {
        cd_collection = realloc(cd_collection, sizeof(CD) * numrecs);
        numrecsread = fread(cd_collection, sizeof(CD), numrecs, f);
        if (numrecsread != numrecs) {
            printf("Error: %d records in file but %d were read into memory",
                         numrecs, numrecsread);
        }
        fclose(f);
    }
    cdarraylen = numrecsread;
    return numrecsread;
}
```

Notice that this function is `static` because I want it to be 'private' within this code-file. The code begins by calling another function `number_of_records_in_db()` which returns the number of records stored in the data file. I'll explain how it does this shortly. Then it tries to open the file in binary read (`"rb"`) mode. If this operation is unsuccessful the return value assigned to `f` is `NULL` and I display an error message. Otherwise, `f` is assigned a pointer to the file.

I read in all the data from the file using `fread()`:

```
numrecsread = fread(cd_collection, sizeof(CD), numrecs, f);
```

The first argument, `cd_collection`, is the array (as mentioned earlier, it is actually a pointer to a `CD struct`) into which the records will be read. The second argument is the size of each item. Each block of data represents a single `CD struct` so I calculate its size as `sizeof(CD)`. The third argument is the number of items to be read and the fourth argument is the file pointer (the pointer to the `FILE struct`). The returned value is the number of items that were read in and this is assigned to the `numrecsread` variable.

This gives me a way of testing that the number of items which I *tried* to read and the number of items that I *actually* read are the same. If they are not the same (due to some unforeseen error), I display an error message:

```
if (numrecsread != numrecs) {
    printf("Error: %d records in file but %d were read into memory",
            numrecs, numrecsread);
}
```

When I've finished processing the file, I close it:

```
fclose(f);
```

But how did I calculate the number of records that were in the file before I began reading them? Recall that this value was stored in `numrecs` and I used this variable in two places. As mentioned above, I used it with `fread()` to specify the number of records to read into the array `cd_collection`:

```
fread(cd_collection, sizeof(CD), numrecs, f);
```

But before I did that I used it in this line of code:

```
cd_collection = realloc(cd_collection, sizeof(CD) * numrecs);
```

In previous example programs the `cd_collection` array was declared to be of a fixed length. For example, if I wanted to store 4 `structs` in the array, I declared the array as:

```
cd_collection[4]
```

But in this program I don't know how many `structs` I need to store until I calculate how many records exist in the file on disk. It could be 4 or it could be 400. And I need some way of setting aside enough memory for `cd_collection` to accommodate all the records read in from the file.

To do this I use the `realloc()` function. We've used `malloc()` previously to allocate memory for an array. In *ReadFile*, I allocated enough memory to store characters read from a file in the char array, `b`, where `size` was the size in bytes or characters of the file:

```
b = malloc(size);
```

Similarly, in the current project, *CDdatabase*, I use `malloc()` in `create_cdcollection()` to set aside enough space for four `CD structs` like this:

```
cd_collection = malloc(sizeof(CD) * 4);
```

The `realloc()` function reallocates (re-uses) memory that was previously allocated using `malloc()`. This allows me to change the amount of memory allocated. But this still doesn't explain how I calculated the number of records in the data file. This was done by this function:

(CDdatabase) cddb.c

```
int number_of_records_in_db(char *filename) {
    FILE *f;
    int endpos;
    int numrecs = 0;

    f = fopen(filename, "rb");
    if (f == NULL) {
        printf("Cannot open file: %s\n", filename);
    } else {
        fseek(f , 0 , SEEK_END);
        endpos = ftell(f);
        numrecs = endpos / sizeof(CD);
        fclose(f);
    }
    return numrecs;
}
```

This function 'moves' the `FILE` pointer, `f`, to the end of the file:

```
fseek(f, 0, SEEK_END);
```

It calls the `ftell()` function to return the position of the file pointer. The 'position' of the end of the file is, in effect, the total size of the file. My code assigns this value to the `endpos` variable. In order to calculate the number of records in the file, I just need to divide the size of the file, `endpos`, by the size of a single `CD` record. This tells me how many `CD` records fit into a file of this size. This is how I do that calculation:

```
numrecs = endpos / sizeof(CD);
```

The function `load_cdcollection()`, which is shown in full earlier in this chapter, is responsible for loading records previously saved to disk and recreating the `CD` structs in memory:

```
cd_collection = realloc(cd_collection, sizeof(CD) * numrecs)
numrecsread = fread(cd_collection, sizeof(CD), numrecs, f);
```

When `CD` records are loaded from a file into the `cd_collection` array, the total number of records is saved in the variable `cdarraylen` (declared in *cddb.h*):

```
cdarraylen = numrecsread;
```

This variable is used later when I save the records from the array into a disk file in the `save_cdcollection()` function.

In my program, I save this data into a backup file called "*cd_database.bak*". The data-saving routine is very straightforward. First I open the file in binary write (`"wb"`) mode. Then I use `fwrite()` to save data from `cd_collection` with each item having the size of a `CD struct`, and the total number of items given by `cdarraylen`:

```
fwrite(cd_collection, sizeof(CD), cdarraylen, f);
```

The rest of the code in this short function (on the following page) is used to check that the operation has completed correctly, then the file is closed and some messages are displayed:

CDdatabase (cddb.c)

```
void save_cdcollection(char *filename) {
    FILE *f;
    int count;

    f = fopen(filename, "wb");
    if (f == NULL) {
        printf("Cannot write to file: %s\n", filename);
    } else {
        count = fwrite(cd_collection, sizeof(CD), cdarraylen, f);
        if (count != cdarraylen) {
            printf("initialization failed\n");
        } else {
            printf("saved\n");
        }
        fclose(f);
    }
}
```

To add a new `CD` to the data file, I call `add_cd()`. This function begins by calling my `readcd_data()` function which prompts the user to enter data for each field of a `CD` record, converts strings to integers when appropriate and does a bit of simple error checking. At the end of all that it initializes the fields of a global `CD struct` called `tempcd`:

```
strcpy(tempcd.name, cdname);
strcpy(tempcd.artist, cdartist);
tempcd.trackcount = tracknum;
tempcd.rating = ratingnum;
```

To add the new data stored in `tempcd` to the existing data file, the `add_cd()` function opens the file in binary append mode (`"ab"`) and calls `fwrite()` to write one `CD`'s worth of data into it:

CDdatabase (cddb.c)

```
void add_cd(char *filename) {
    FILE *f;

    readcd_data();
    f = fopen(filename, "ab");
    if (f == 0) {
        printf("Cannot write to file: %s\n", filename);
    } else {
        fwrite(&tempcd, sizeof(CD), 1, f);
        fclose(f);
    }
}
```

Notice, by the way, that `fwrite()` requires its first argument to be the *address* of the data to be written. When I called `fwrite()` previously, that argument was `cd_collection` – which is an array. In C, an array is an address in memory, so it needs no special syntax when used with `fwrite()`. With a `struct`, however, I need to pass the address of the `struct` which is why I have had to use the ampersand (`&`) 'address-of' operator: `&tempcd`.

Finally, I want to look at the code needed to find a specific CD record in the file and modify the data which it contains. This begins with the `modify_cd()` function. This function prompts the user to enter the number of a CD – that is, the index of the CD in the data file, where 0 indicates the first CD.

There is a minor problem here. I need to convert the string entered by the user to a number using the `atoi()` function. That function returns 0 to indicate an error when it is unable to convert the string. But in this case, 0 is a valid number when the user enters it to mean the first record at index 0. My solution is to treat the character '0' as a special case and flag an error by setting an `error` variable to 1 when `atoi()` returns 0:

```
if (input[0] == '0') {
cdnum = 0;
} else {
    cdnum = atoi(input);
    if (cdnum  == 0) {
        error = 1;
    }
}
```

This is the full code of the `modify_cd()` function which is found in the *cddb.c* code file in the *CDdatabase* project:

CDdatabase (cddb.c)

```
void modify_cd(char *filename) {
    char input[MAXSTRLEN];
    int cdnum;
    int slen;
    int error = 0;

    printf("Enter CD Number to modify:\n> ");
    slen = readln(input);
    if (slen > 0) {
        if (input[0] == '0') {
            cdnum = 0;
        } else {
            cdnum = atoi(input);
            if (cdnum == 0) {
                error = 1;
            }
        }
```

CDdatabase (cddb.c - continued)

```
    } else {
        error = 1;
    };
    if (error) {
        printf("Error: invalid number!\n");
    } else if ((cdnum < 0) || (cdnum > (number_of_records_in_db(filename) - 1)))
{
        printf("Error: Cannot find cd number %d\n", cdnum);
    } else {
        change_cd(filename, cdnum);
    }
}
```

After a bit more error-checking the `modify_cd()` function calls `change_cd()` – and that is where the real work is done. This function opens the file in binary read-and-write mode (`"rb+"`) It allocates enough memory for a single `CD` record and assigns this to a `CD` pointer `cdptr`:

```
cdptr = malloc(sizeof(CD));
```

It then seeks to a position in the file given by the integer `cdnum`. For example, if `cdnum` were 0 it would seek to the first `CD` record (at index 0), if `cdnum` were 7 it would seek to the eighth `CD` record (at index 7).

In order to seek to the appropriate position it multiplies `cdnum` by the size of a `CD` record. This moves the file-pointer by the correct number of bytes through the file:

```
fseek(f, cdnum * sizeof(CD), SEEK_SET);
```

The final argument, the constant `SEEK_SET`, specifies that the starting point of the seek operation is the beginning of the file. My code then reads in one `CD`'s worth of data from the current position in the file:

```
r = fread(cdptr, sizeof(CD), 1, f);
```

Now my `readcd_data()` function is called to prompt the user to enter some new data for the `CD` record. As before, this data is stored in `tempcd`. And finally the data from `tempcd` is copied into the `struct` pointed to by `cdptr`:

```
strcpy(cdptr->name, tempcd.name);
strcpy(cdptr->artist, tempcd.artist);
cdptr->trackcount = tempcd.trackcount;
cdptr->rating = tempcd.rating;
```

Then I seek again to the position of the record which I want to modify and save the new data at that position. As `cdptr` is a pointer variable I can pass this as the first argument to `fwrite()` without having to precede it with the `&` address-of operator:

```
r = fseek(f, cdnum * sizeof(CD), SEEK_SET);
r = fwrite(cdptr, sizeof(CD), 1, f);
```

This is the full code of the `change_cd()` function:

CDdatabase (cddb.c)

```
static void change_cd(char *filename, int cdnum) {
    FILE *f;
    CD* cdptr;
    size_t r;

    f = fopen(filename, "rb+");
    if (f == NULL) {
        printf("Cannot open file: %s\n", filename)
    } else {
        cdptr = (CD*)malloc(sizeof(CD));
        r = fseek(f, cdnum * sizeof(CD), SEEK_SET);
        r = fread(cdptr, sizeof(CD), 1, f);
        readcd_data();
        strcpy(cdptr->name, tempcd.name);
        strcpy(cdptr->artist, tempcd.artist);
        cdptr->trackcount = tempcd.trackcount;
        cdptr->rating = tempcd.rating;
        r = fseek(f, cdnum * sizeof(CD), SEEK_SET);
        r = fwrite(cdptr, sizeof(CD), 1, f);
        fclose(f);
    }
}
```

The -> Operator

The end result is that I have written new data fields into the record at the specified position in my data file. There is just one more thing here that needs to be explained. What are those `->` operators? It turns out that they are provided for the purpose of accessing the fields of a `struct` to which a pointer is pointing. When you use a `struct` variable such as `tempcd` you can access its fields using a dot, like this:

```
tempcd.name
```

But when you have a *pointer* to a `struct` such as `cdptr` you access the fields using the `->` operator like this:

```
cdptr->name
```

And Finally ...

So we finally come to the end of this little book. Over the last ten chapters we have covered a lot of ground. If you have followed from the beginning you should now be well-equipped to write C programs and understand other people's C programs. There is, of course, much more that you can learn about C – and the most important thing you can do to increase your understanding of C programming is to write lots of C programs. The adventure is only just beginning – where it goes next is up to you!

Appendix

Here is a brief reference to elements of the C language plus some useful resources for writing and compiling C programs.

Elements of the C Language

Types

When your programs do calculations or display some text, they use data. The data items each have a data type. For example, to do calculations you may use integer numbers such as 10. Each type has a name such as `int` for an integer (a whole number) or `char` for a single character.

Variables

A variable is a named piece of data. A variable name can include alphabetic characters, numbers and underscores. The first character of the name cannot be a number. When declaring a variable, you must put the type first, then the variable name like this:

```
int x;
```

The value of a variable can be changed (which is why it is called a variable). So my integer variable `x` could be given the value 10 and then, later on, given the value 100 like this:

```
x = 10;
x = 100;
```

Functions

Typically we will divide our code into small named blocks or 'functions'. The names of functions must be followed by a pair of parentheses like this:

```
void myfunction()
```

The start and end of a function is indicated with a pair of curly brackets and the code of the function is placed between those brackets, like this:

```
void myfunction() {
}
```

Arguments

Bits of data ('arguments') can be sent to a function. The function must declare those arguments in the form of named 'parameters'. Multiple parameters are separated by commas. The parameters are assigned the values of the arguments passed to the function. Just like variables, parameters must be preceded by their types like this:

```
int add(int num1, int num2)
```

Function Returns

When a function needs to return a piece of data to the code that called the function, the data type must precede the function name. The data to be returned must be placed after the `return` keyword. This function takes two `int` arguments and returns an `int`:

```
int add(int num1, int num2) {
    num1 = num1 + num2;
    return num1;
}
```

When a function does not return any data, its return type is declared to be `void`:

```
void sayHello() {
    printf("Hello\n");
}
```

Keywords

C defines a number of keywords that mean special things to the language. You cannot use these keywords as the names of variables or functions. Keywords include words such as `return`, `if`, `else`, `for`, `while` and the names of data types such as `char`, `double` and `int`.

Statements

A statement is a small piece of code such as an assignment or a function call. In C, single statements are terminated with a semicolon `;` character. Here, for example, are four statements, each terminated with a semicolon:

```
printf("Hello world");
sayHello();
greet("Mary");
x = 100;
```

When you need several statements to execute one after another – for example, when some test evaluates to *true* (here I test if the `num` variable has a value of 100), you may enclose the statements between a pair of curly brackets, like this:

```
if (num == 100){
    printf("Hello world");
    sayHello();
    greet("Mary");
    x = 100;
}
```

Operators

Operators are special symbols that are used to do operations such as adding numbers, comparing two values or assigning a value to a variable. Here I declare an `int` variable `n` and set its value to 10 using the `=` 'assignment operator':

```
n = 10;
```

Here I use the addition operator `+` to add 2 to 10. The resulting value (12) is then assigned to the variable `n`:

```
n = 2 + 10;
```

And here I test if `n` is less than 10 using the 'less than' operator `<` and only if `n` is less than 10 do I run the code to show "Hello world":

```
if (n < 10) {
    printf("Hello world");
}
```

Directives

C has a number of special directives preceded by a hash '#' character such as `#include` and `#define`. These directives are instructions to a C tool called the pre-processor which makes changes to your code before it is translated into runnable machine-code by the C compiler.

Comments

Comments can be added to your programs to describe what each section is supposed to do. Comments are not treated as runnable code. C lets you insert multi-line comments between pairs of `/*` and `*/` delimiters, like this:

```
/* This program displays any
 * arguments that were passed to it */
```

In addition to these multi-line comments, modern C compilers also let you use 'line comments' that begin with two slash characters `//` and extend to the end of the current line. Line comments may either comment out an entire line or any part of a line which may include code before the `//` characters. These are examples of line comments:

```
// This is a full-line comment

for (i = 0; i < argc; i++)     // part-line comment
```

C IDEs and Editors

There are numerous IDEs (integrated development environments) and source code editors that support the C language. In most cases, the developers and users of these IDEs will provide tutorials on their installation and usage. There are also many tutorials on YouTube. No attempt is made in this book to duplicate any of those tutorials (indeed, if I had done so, this would quickly have become *The Huge Book of C* rather than the little one you are now reading). So, I assume at the outset that you have downloaded and installed an appropriate IDE and taken the time to become familiar with its basic features.

There are some popular free cross-platform C IDEs such as CodeLite and Code::Blocks. On Windows, both C++Builder and Microsoft's Visual Studio are good choices for C development. The most widely used Windows IDE is Visual Studio. However, many Visual Studio users don't know how to get started with C programming, as there is no C project type. If you need some help, refer to the section in this appendix on *Getting Started with Visual Studio.*

Microsoft Visual Studio

https://visualstudio.microsoft.com/vs/community/

C++Builder

https://www.embarcadero.com/products/cbuilder/starter

CodeLite

http://codelite.org/

Code::Blocks

http://www.codeblocks.org/

NetBeans

http://www.netbeans.org/

Komodo Edit

http://www.activestate.com/komodo-edit

Unsafe Functions

In the code that accompanies this book, you will see that I have often used some old or 'traditional' C functions such as `gets()` and `strcpy()`. Some (but not all) C compilers may object to these functions. If your compiler warns you that certain functions are 'unsafe' it may also suggest newer alternatives that you can use in their place.

For example, the Microsoft C compiler in Visual Studio recommends that I use `strcpy_s()` instead of `strcpy()` and, even though it allows me to use `gets()`, it warns me that the function is 'undefined' because it is not found in the supplied header file.

Why Old Functions?

In this book, I decided to use old functions such as `gets()` and `strcpy()`for two reasons:

1. These functions work with most modern C compilers even if they may sometimes generate warnings, whereas some of the newer and safer alternative functions are not supported by all compilers .
2. You will see these functions in innumerable books, online sites, legacy code and C code examples, so every C programmer needs to be familiar with them.

Most of the old and 'unsafe' functions are related to string-handling. As you will know by now, C strings are much harder to deal with than strings in most other modern languages (such as Java, C#, Python, Pascal or Ruby) for the simple reason that C doesn't define a string data-type. A string is just a memory location where some characters are stored. It is up to the programmer to ensure that the memory location is correct and that sufficient memory is allocated for a string of a certain length.

C Standards

There are several standards that define the C language. C has evolved over the forty or more years of its existence. The first 'standard' was the book by Brian W. Kernighan and Dennis M. Ritchie, "The C programming Language". This wasn't really a standard – it just described Dennis Ritchie's implementation of C at the time (1978). The first real standard was ANSI (American National Standards Institute) C in 1989 (sometimes called C89). This is *the* standard that most C code is based on, even today: all currently active C compilers fully support ANSI C.

The next standard was C99 (1999) which introduced, among other things, `bool` (Boolean) and `long long int` (64-bit integer) types and the single line comment `//`. Not all compilers fully support C99, though all (that I'm aware of) support the `//` comment.

Then came C11 (2011) which introduced more new features and removed `gets()`. There are some compilers that claim to implement this standard fully. However, two of the most widely used compilers, GNU and Microsoft C/C++, do not. Microsoft C/C++ is less C11 compatible than GNU, which claims to be "substantially complete". The latest standard is C18 which is really a bug-fix and clarification of C11. It does not introduce any new language features.

In Microsoft C/C++ you will find 'secure' string handling routines like `strcpy_s()`. These were included as an optional part of the C11 standard and are not implemented by many C compilers.

In this book, I have mostly used ANSI C (technically, it's called ISO C90, since ANSI no longer has anything to do with it) as the definition of the C language that I am describing. The other standards are really fairly minor revisions of ANSI C. If you want to write code that is portable between compilers and operating systems, then stick to ANSI C.

Dealing With Compiler Warnings

For the purposes of this book, you may usually ignore any warnings from your compiler stating that a function is unsafe or 'deprecated' (in programming terms when a function is deprecated its use is not recommended and it is possible that the function itself may be removed at some future date). In your own programs, however, it would probably be best to substitute safer functions when your compiler shows a warning. You should consult your compiler's documentation for recommended alternatives. Be aware, however, that some of these alternatives may not be 100% compatible with other compilers on other operating systems.

Alternatively, in some cases, you may decide to write your own functions. This is what I did, for example, when I wrote the `readln()` function in Chapter 4, as a safer alternative to `gets()` and `fgets()`.

In some cases, the warnings or errors may result from certain compiler options being set. Your IDE may let you change the compiler options so that your projects target certain standards of the C language such as ANSI C, C99 or C11. Different standards may be more or less strict in permitting the use of certain functions.

You may also have the option of hash-defining symbols in your code in order to disable warnings. In Visual Studio, for example, I can disable warnings about many 'unsafe' functions by defining the pre-processor macro `_CRT_SECURE_NO_WARNINGS` in a Visual Studio property sheet or adding this at the top of the code file:

```
#define _CRT_SECURE_NO_WARNINGS
```

What About scanf()?

The `scanf()` function provides another common way of getting user input. While `scanf()` is widely used, you may notice that I have never used it in the code accompanying this book. Why is that? After all, `scanf()` seems like the obvious partner function to `printf()`. You can use `printf()` to display a given number of data elements each of which must have a specific data type. And you can use `scanf()` to read in a given number of data elements each of which must have a specific data type.

However, there is a big difference. When you use `printf()` in your programs, the number and type of data elements to be displayed are largely under your control. You can check that they are all valid before displaying them. But when you read data (either from the console or from a file) you are relying on someone else (the user entering data or the person who created the file) to provide correct data. If you use `scanf()` to read in the wrong data by mistake it can potentially cause catastrophic program crashes. For that reason, `scanf()` is generally regarded as a hazardous function. It may be better to read in ordinary string data with `fgets()` or a similar function and then parse out the data items in your code. This obviously requires more work than using `scanf()` but it is also safer.

Getting Started With Visual Studio

Windows programmers may use Microsoft Visual Studio to create C projects. In order to do so, you must be sure to install support for C++ projects. You may either use a commercial or a free edition of Visual Studio.

Visual Studio Community is the free edition. It includes support for programming languages including C, C++, C#, HTML/JavaScript, and Visual Basic. It is free for students, open source development, individual developers (creating free or paid-for applications) and small teams. Refer to the Terms & Conditions on the Microsoft site. Download here: https://visualstudio.microsoft.com/vs/community/

To create a C project, follow these steps:

- Select the *File* menu, then *New* | *Project*
- In the *New Project* window select *Visual C++* (on the left – this may be listed under 'Other Languages') then *General* and (on the right) select *Empty Project*
- Name the project, and browse to a location on disk
- Click *OK*

Visual Studio now creates a new project with separate folders for Header Files, Resource Files and Source Files.

How to Add a New C file to a Visual Studio Project

- Right-click the *Source Files* folder.
- From the popup menu, select *Add* | *New Item*
- Select *Code* | *C++ (.cpp) file.*

You will need to edit the default file name.
In the *Name* field, change the file name to: *main.c*
Click *Add.*

Edit the contents of this source file to the following:

```
#include <stdio.h>

int main(){
    printf("Hello world\n");
    return 0;
}
```

Keeping the Visual Studio Console Visible

To prevent the console from vanishing before you've had time to see the output, add a breakpoint by clicking in the grey margin to the left of this code line:

```
return 0;
```

A red dot should appear in the margin. Save the file and run (and debug) the application by pressing F5.

How to Add an Existing C File to the Project

You can also create new projects from existing code by adding code files. Right-click the *Source Files* folder in the Solution Explorer and select *Add | Existing Item*. Naturally, header files should be added to the *Header* folder.

Web Sites

There are innumerable web sites that contain information and tutorials about the C language. Here are some sites that you may find useful.

Microsoft C Runtime Library Reference

http://msdn.microsoft.com/en-us/library/59ey50w6.aspx

Tutorialspoint C Standard Library Reference

http://www.tutorialspoint.com/c_standard_library/stdlib_h.htm

Bitwise Courses

Bitwise Courses is the online site for interactive programming tutorials on C, C#, Java, Object Pascal and other languages. These tutorials are made by the publishers of Bitwise Books. For more information – and special offers – on my programming courses, be sure to visit the Bitwise Courses web site:

http://www.bitwisecourses.com/

Using the Source Code

The source code of all the projects described in this book can be downloaded from the Bitwise Books web site:

http://www.bitwisebooks.com

The code is provided in a Zip archive and you will need to unzip the archive in order to extract the code into directories on your disk. The code is supplied as single Visual Studio Solution which, on Windows, can be loaded directly into Microsoft Visual Studio. If you haven't got a copy of Visual Studio, you can download a free copy here:

https://visualstudio.microsoft.com/vs/community/

If you are using some other C programming editor or IDE, you will need to create a project in the usual way and either load the supplied C source code files into the project or simply copy and paste the code into your main C file.

In most cases, the C code should compile without errors when using any standard C compiler on Windows, Mac or Linux. In some cases, as we have used some 'old' C functions, you may see warnings or you may need to set options to permit the use of functions which your compiler considers to be 'unsafe'. We have used these functions for reasons of compatibility (newer and 'safer' functions may not be supported by all compilers). In your own projects you would probably prefer to use whichever functions are recommended by your compiler. For the purposes of this book, this is not an important consideration, however.

Little Books Of ...

The Little Book Of C is one of a series of '*Little Books Of* ...' for programmers. In each *Little Book* we aim to give you *just the stuff you really need* to get straight to the heart of the matter without all the fluff and padding.

We know that there is plenty of information online about standard code libraries, so we don't fill the pages of these books by duplicating that information. Instead, we aim to explain the really important details that you need to gain a solid understanding of each subject and start hands-on programming as quickly as possible.

Other '*Little Books Of* ...' are:

The Little Book of Pointers
An in-depth guide to pointers in C:

- Indirection
- Pointer arithmetic
- Data Alignment
- Linked Lists (single/double)
- Stacks & Queues
- Function Pointers
- Common Pointer Problems

The Little Book of Recursion
Understanding recursion techniques in C:

- Recursive Functions
- The Call Stack
- Stack Frames
- Stack Corruption
- Recursion & Scope
- Tree Structures
- Disk Directory Recursion

You can also download some useful free resources from the Bitwise Books web site:

http://www.bitwisebooks.com

Made in United States
Orlando, FL
10 November 2026

90510169R00083